Designs
for elBulli and Sketches

Luki Huber

Grub Street . London

Contents

Foreword

Ferran Adrià

Endless exploration

I met Luki Huber during the first winter of working at elBulli workshop, when my brother Albert got in contact with him to order a few designs. Soon, what was meant to be a collaborative experience where he would be working *for* us turned into a formula that allowed him to work *with* us. Luki was very important, because he became a part of the inception of the first haute cuisine workshop in history, with all that this would come to signify. And from then on, until 2005, his presence was felt each season in all of the creativity that went into elBulli.

With Luki we were able to create, right from the very start, a system for work that was marked by immediacy and efficiency, thanks to the fact that we were working as a team. This type of relationship helped to bring about a change in the traditional dynamic of how a restaurant worked. Until then, the chef, or restaurateur, would go to a shop to buy an already designed plate. However, we now began to design everything we needed, with everything that this process involved: the design of containers for special preparations or dishes; or the opposite: the creation of preparations that could highlight some brilliant design concept. What's more, Luki began to think up and propose objects that were not only for serving and holding food, but which could be used to achieve totally new preparations or to enhance other already existing ones.

Our partnership bore fruit practically every day for more than three years, the result of an incredible rapport between his way of thinking and ours. Endless exploration, shouting out ideas, and never being afraid to reject what might be considered a great idea. In a way, Luki was a kind of soul mate, someone with whom we were able to fully capitalise on the extraordinary immediacy that haute cuisine demands. And in order to make this possible, in addition to his fathomless talent, Luki had an essential trait: he was always aware that the food had to come first, not the object he had designed. This attitude made our collaboration exceptionally smooth.

A consequence of this attitude was the attention he drew from the organisers of the design exhibition held at the Centre Georges Pompidou in Paris in 2005, where together with Luki we presented *elBulli creative methods*. The exhibition featured the serving objects we had created together, and a small sample of the objects we used to prepare food, i.e. to cook with. The following year, I became the first chef and the first Spaniard to receive the Lucky Strike Design Award, an acknowledgement that had previously been awarded to such figures as Philippe Starck, Karl Lagerfeld and Donna Karan. Naturally, I considered it to be recognition of what interdisciplinary dialogue can come to signify. Evidently, I'm not a designer, but our activity turned out to be the ideal platform for design. As I never

customise its own design. Luki's career has gone on to thrive brilliantly, first through the design of culinary utensils, which I believe has come out of his time with elBulli. And later with Manual Thinking, a wonderful discovery which, I like to believe, may have something to do with our intense exchanges regarding the best way of organising our work and our creative tasks.

Going over the pages of this book has taken me back to an exciting time, one in which we would look forward to Luki arriving from Barcelona with new ideas, with contributions that were always stimulating, fun and brilliant. I hope the readers of this book will also enjoy the designs that fill its pages, and be able to capture the special atmosphere that was to be experienced in Cala Montjoi during those four years.

cease to say, the award was given to Ferran Adrià, but had it not been for this very close and intense partnership with Luki Huber, it might not have happened.

Since 2006, we've continued to collaborate, on certain occasions, and I've also been in talks with other designers. But we've never repeated (nor have we entertained the thought) the winning formula we'd created, that allowed a small business like elBulli to

Still life created by the team at elBulli for the
De Dietrich Dialogue exhibition in 2007.
The displayed items encapsulate some of
the results of the collaboration between
Luki Huber and Ferran Adrià.

A conversation with Ferran Adrià and Luki Huber

Trinitat Gilbert

Have you ever seen a plastic pipette, one you find in a science lab, used as a skewer for food, such as a cherry tomato and cheese? The pipette contains a sauce, which you inject into the food at will. What a simple and at the same time visually striking idea!

Do you have tweezers at home, the typical ones found in a laboratory, that you use for eating ham? Or better yet, have you ever had them given to you as cutlery in a restaurant? Tweezers allow Westerners to handle their food more skilfully than they would when eating with chopsticks.

The most gastronomically inclined among you are sure to have a straining spoon for eating cereal, keeping its contents moist but without the liquid, which will have drained through its many holes. As you use it, have you ever stopped to wonder how on earth this idea could have occurred to anyone?

Luki Huber, the industrial designer, has the answer. But it didn't occur to him on his own. Nor did he work alone. Luki was a member of the Beatles of cuisine, i.e. elBulli, and together they designed utensils with which to compose the most radical culinary music. Those utensils were ground-breaking in themselves. Never before had anyone thought that the implements used in a laboratory could be used in a kitchen. And Luki and Ferran and Albert Adrià continue to pose the question, 'why not?'

elBulli revolutionised cooking. This is the phrase/sentence/cliché used when speaking about the restaurant that was located in Cala Montjoi, in the town of Roses, which was run by Ferran Adrià and Juli Soler. That said, the cooking techniques themselves were always the same. elBulli didn't invent steaming. Or tempura. Or boiling. To name three. What did it do then, for us to happily state that in that hidden cove of Roses reached by a winding road, such a radical change was cooked up?

The 'codi Bulli', as Ferran Adrià puts it, the revolution, consisted of taking nothing for granted, asking questions about everything, feeling passion for work, taking risks and, more importantly, sharing knowledge with the world.

Juli Soler, Albert Adrià, Oriol Castro and Luki Huber (left to right) together in the kitchen at the elBulli workshop.

View of elBulli on the cove of Cala Montjoi.

Luki Huber in 2003 in front of the restaurant.

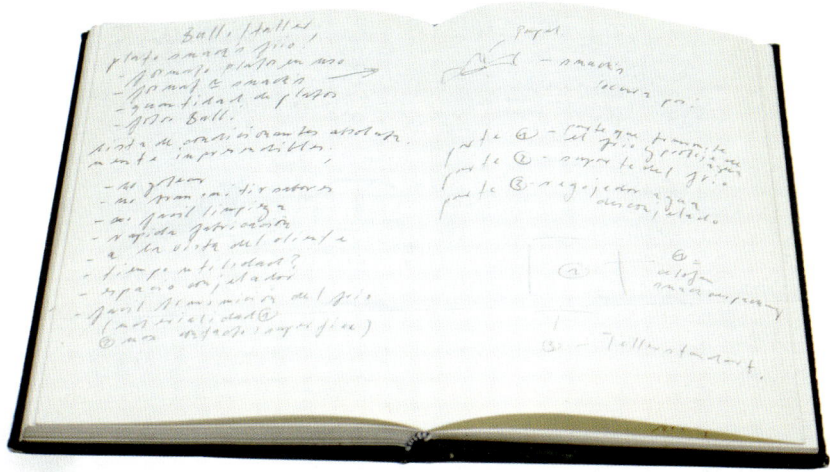

The first page of Luki Huber's first sketch book, dedicated to his collaboration with elBulli.

The industrial designer Luki Huber fell into the category of 'taking risks'. 'He made molecular cuisine possible; he was the one to put it into practice,' says Ferran Adrià while pointing to Luki, originally from Switzerland, who has lived in Barcelona for twenty-five years.

He was twenty-six when he met Albert Adrià, and it marked a turning point in his career. In fact, it was Albert Adrià who put his trust in Luki, after a casual meeting, to think up a way of serving frozen desserts at the table without letting them melt.

It was then that they took the next step. The revolutionary step. An industrial designer joined the elBulli workforce. With a fixed salary. Just like a chef.

In practice, however, there was no assigned space for Luki at elBulli, in Cala Montjoi. 'Just like Ferran, I had no set place in the kitchen,' he says. And as he had no set place, he moved around, practising Ferran Adrià's famous 'vaig i vinc' technique, meaning that he would come and go around the restaurant as he pleased. As he walked, he would try to think up solutions for the problems facing the chefs.

Luki's role was to find design solutions that would allow chefs' theories to be put into practice. Where this point is concerned, Luki plays down his importance, but Ferran stresses it. They made a united team, with such respect for one another that it would be difficult to determine who did what. Together, they wrote the opening

For the 1998 season, elBulli commissioned Esther San Millán, Rafa Mateo and Miguel Gascó to design a set of silver plates for serving petit fours.

The atypical use of kitchen utensils began a quest to find or design new appliances and utensils. Before Ferran created his famous foams, the siphon was only used to whip cream.

Pipette, tweezers and FACES straining spoon.

Drop-by-drop – caviar maker.

pages of the story of the marriage between gastronomy and design. 'It was like a game of ping-pong,' Luki insists. A metaphor to describe how work was done and undone as a team.

Let's look at some examples. Take spherification. 'Blame Luki for us using syringes,' says Ferran. Luki clearly recalls the occasion. Albert Adrià wanted to make melon caviar and to have it look like the caviar you get from a sturgeon. They would be made using syringes, so that the droplets could fall, one at a time, into a solution of calcium chloride. The longer the droplet remained in the solution, the thicker the skin of the resulting pearl would become. As the droplets fell in succession, there was a realisation that some had a

pleasant texture similar to that of caviar. The droplets that came out first had an overly thick skin, while the last to come out had an overly thin skin.

Luki thought that if you arranged a number of syringes simultaneously pointing downwards and allowed them to drip melon juice mixed with sodium alginate into the solution, the result would be even.

As soon as the customers were seated at elBulli, the waiters would tell the chefs the exact number of plates of melon caviar they had to prepare, and then the syringes would be put to work.

Luki Huber problem-solver had ironed out yet another problem. Oh! And he had also

Science and Gastronomy still life created
for the _De Dietrich Dialogue_ exhibition.

Presentation of the FACES range at Vinçon,
Barcelona. Group photo with Miquel de Mas,
Miquel Cunill, Xavier Claramunt, Neus Canal,
Luki Huber, Ferran Adrià, Martin de Azúa, Gerard
Moliné, Antoni Arola and Jordi Tamayo.

invented the name. Ferran asked him to think up names for this new technique, and among the proposals noted down was 'spherification'. Ferran would always ask for lots of proposals so that he could later choose the best one.

Another example is molecular cuisine. Ferran insists that the molecular cuisine practised at elBulli was only possible thanks to Luki. And he adds: 'He paved the way to what would become ground-breaking food design.' It was so ground-breaking that design schools today offer the subject of Food Design. It is likely that without the paradigm shift brought about through the association between Albert Adrià, Luki Huber and Ferran Adrià, such university-level studies would never have been considered.

Whatever the case, how did Luki make the molecular cuisine the Adriàs were after possible?

While walking down Barcelona's Via Laietana, Luki saw a shop selling a watering system consisting of thin PVC hoses. And as he observed the whimsical shapes the different hoses made, he thought of the jelly noodles they were making at elBulli. The noodles were made in a specific way, but perhaps the same could be done using those hoses to make them cylindrical, as spaghetti.

Spherical olives presented on a snack spoon from the FACES range.

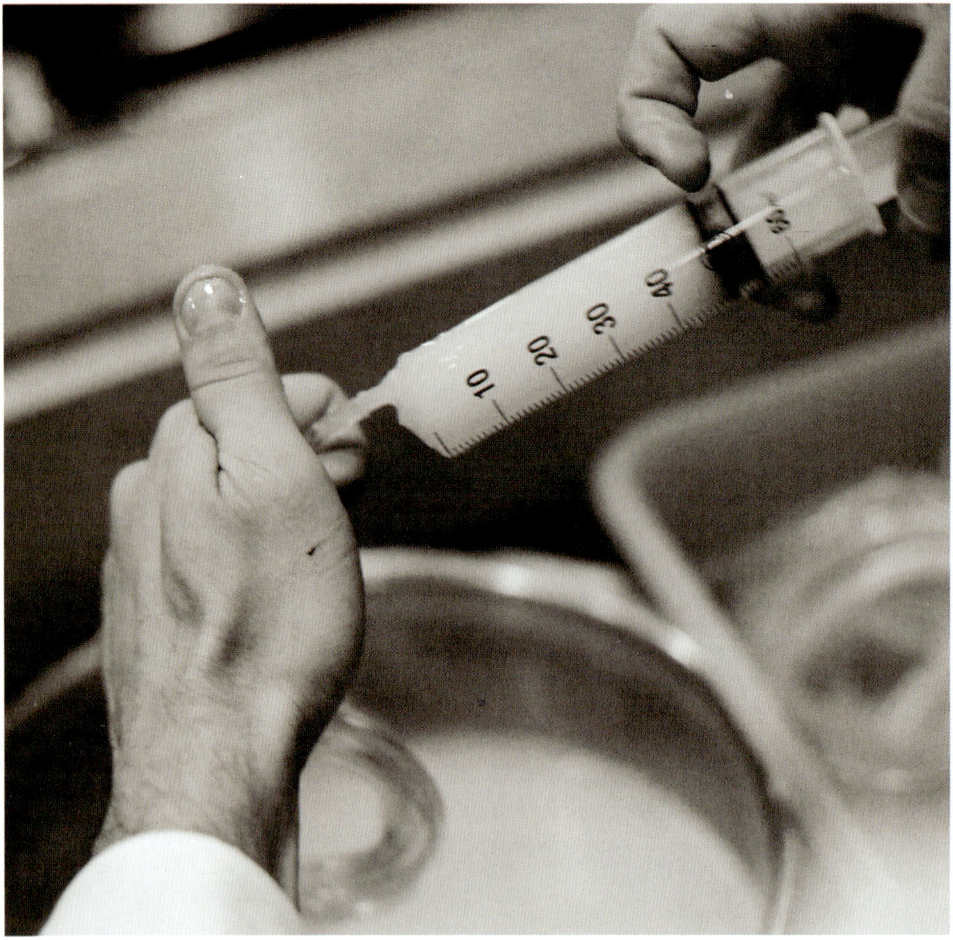

Making a Parmesan *spaghetto*.

Ferran Adrià, Luki Huber and Marc Cuspinera making a last-minute check before the opening of the *Ferran Adrià: Notes on Creativity* exhibition at the Drawing Center in New York.

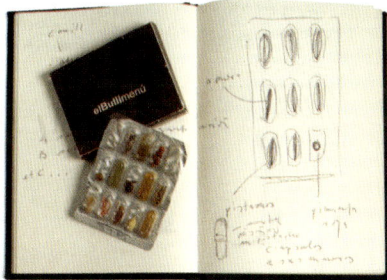

Sketch books on display at the *Ferran Adrià: Notes on Creativity* exhibition. The display cases feature the books with the sketches and the prototypes made of the designs.

Luki took the hoses to elBulli, where they were filled with Parmesan water into which agar-agar had been dissolved. When cooled, the mixture set. And vollà, the first jelly *spaghetto* was made. It was called a *spaghetto* (the singular form of spaghetti) because each diner was served only one, but it was two metres in length.

With the jelly *spaghetto* set inside the hose, they achieved molecular cuisine as it had been defined in 1969 by the scientists Hervé This and Nicholas Kurti when they associated scientific principles with home cooking, but nobody would be able to eat it without first taking it out of the hose, for which then an effective system hadn't been developed.

Luki attempted everything possible. Some of his ideas were immediately ruled out, such as cutting open the hose, because the *spaghetto* would break, and because the hose could never be remade. He even tried using a bicycle pump, but it was not feasible. Mainly for reasons of hygiene.

Finally, he found the solution. He built an adapter for a kitchen siphon or cream whipper, which injected pressurised air, expelling the jelly *spaghetto*.

That was how the most creative 'ping-pong' team worked. They had the **'*codi Bulli*'** in their heads and, consequently, the freedom with which they worked was completely

Visitors to the *D.Day le design aujourd'hui*
exhibition at the Centre Pompidou in Paris.

Catalogue from the *D.Day* exhibition.

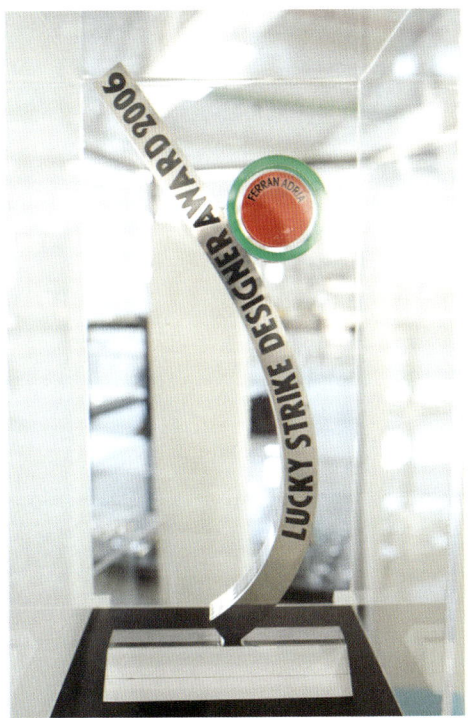

Lucky Strike Designer Award received by Ferran Adrià in 2006 in Berlin.

Objects currently on display at elBulliLab, in Calle de Méjico, Barcelona.

unhindered. **'**Today I advise even business people never to go to industry trade events alone,**'** Huber explains. While working at elBulli, he did go to a laboratory equipment show from which he returned with different ideas.

Specifically, he brought back to the restaurant stainless steel mesh that was originally used for filtering. Luki thought that the mesh could be used to cook in some way, although it was finally used as tableware, with the advantage that these food holders could be shaped by hand, creating a set of tableware with myriad shapes.

It wouldn't be possible to end this section about the industrial designer's work with the Adrià brothers, Juli Soler and the entire elBulli kitchen team without mentioning the Lucky Strike Designer Award received by Ferran Adrià in Berlin in 2006. This highly prestigious acknowledgement is kept by the chef at elBulliLab, in Barcelona's Calle de Méjico, inside a glass display case, which he proudly displays.

Introduction

Luki Huber

My collaboration with elBulli spanned five years, during which time I believe we were able to form a one-of-a-kind 'partnership', a symbiosis between a prestigious and well-established, avant-garde, fine-dining restaurant and an industrial designer who was actually only just starting out on his career. Why did we succeed in creating this highly fruitful dialogue that lasted so long? Most likely it was because there was a conjunction of circumstances, coincidences, compatible personalities, a mutual ability to adapt, flexibility, passion...

But let's take it one step at a time. This is surely the best way to explain how our collaboration came about. Albert Adrià was the one who opened the doors of elBulli to me, with a very specific commission: to design a container for serving frozen snacks. How did we meet? That was the first coincidence. It all began with a phone call from my uncle, who worked as a graphic designer for Delicatessa, the gourmet section of the Globus department stores in Switzerland. It's a department that organises events from time to time, which these types of gourmet establishments often do: themed weeks dedicated to countries, products, etc.

The point is that they were planning a special activity for Spain, which consisted of looking for particular products: La Mancha saffron, canned seafood products from Galicia, ham, oil, etc. This was to be accompanied by a magazine article in which they wanted to include a recipe for sea bream cooked in a salt crust by a Spanish chef. I actually knew very little about cooking. Marta and I would go out to dinner at Chinese restaurants and other modest establishments, gastronomically speaking. My only connection with cuisine was that Marta and I had done a packaging design for the Xocoa company. So I paid a visit to the guys at Xocoa and told them I was looking for a good chef who could make a decent sea bream cooked in a salt crust. They told me that I could find the elBulli workshop close by and that I should ask them if they could recommend anybody to me.

So I went to the elBulli workshop in Carrer de la Portaferrisa in Barcelona and rang the doorbell. I think it was Albert himself who opened the door, and immediately after introducing myself as a designer and saying that I had been sent by Xocoa, they showed me round the whole premises, where they had just moved a few months earlier.

I was completely awestruck, to the point where, when it came to telling them why I had come, I changed the question. Instead of asking them to recommend a chef, I asked whether they could make sea bream cooked in a salt crust for the Delicatessa magazine. It turned out that Ferran, who was there at the time, knew about the gourmet offering at Globus. He said that it was one of the chains that he liked the most of all the ones he knew internationally. And he said yes.

When my uncle relayed the answer to the management at Globus, they were amazed, because they were very familiar with who Ferran Adrià was. In fact, I still have a wonderful relationship and am in regular contact with Globus, despite my uncle no longer working for them. Evidently, they were thrilled to approve the proposal. A while later, they came to Barcelona and spent the afternoon with Ferran at the workshop to do their report. I went with them that day, just to act as an interpreter. As a matter of fact, the sea bream cooked in a salt crust was finally made at Hacienda Benazuza, the restaurant near Seville that elBulli had at the time.

During that session, Albert asked me what I did exactly. Because my studio was in nearby Carrer d'Avinyó, I invited him to come and see me. He did come to my studio and I showed him what I had done until then. I was actually just starting out,

and the only thing I could show him was the packaging for Xocoa and a few candles I had made with Marta, based on origami shapes. And that was how things stayed. Our relations were very cordial, but there was nothing more.

However, Albert phoned me after a few weeks and said: 'Luki, we need a plate for cold snacks. Do you think you can take care of it?' At the time they were making a very fragile frozen pastille, which needed a suitable holder so that it could reach the table intact. I accepted the proposal and we had our first meeting. They explained the problem they were having with the temperature it was made at; they requested a quote; and we arranged the next meeting. I initially dealt with Albert, but Ferran also came to the meetings.

That's how our relationship started, with the proposals I made for materials and holders for this frozen snack.

As it was, however, we would have more meetings, and at each one more proposals would emerge, and Ferran would ask me for a quote each time. For me, this dynamic turned out to be somewhat inconvenient because whenever I returned to the studio after a meeting, I would spend a lot of time writing up quotes instead of designing.

For me, and for them too, it was very convenient that my studio was so close to their workshop, because they would call and I could be there in ten minutes. But I was interested in resolving this 'bureaucratic' matter.

So I brought it up with Ferran. I told him that I could invest my time more efficiently if they gave me all their orders; I could note down my hours and bill them at the end of the month. The truth was that I had very few expenses and could charge them a good price. I'm sure this was an important aspect at the beginning. This system turned out to be suitable for all of us. You never know what to expect in this sort of work, whether you're going to come up with a solution in half an hour or in five days, or whether unexpected expenses will come up. In fact, when some of my designs became successful over time, a number of pastry chefs and restaurateurs would ask me if I could make them ten plates, for instance. But it wasn't feasible. If I was to make a living from this, I would have to charge an extremely high price for the ten plates.

That was the arrangement we had during the first stage of our collaboration, starting in the winter of 2000–2001, and throughout the 2001 season. Later came the elBulli retrospective of 2002, for which designs weren't needed in such a systematic way. But one day, after the results of 2001 came out, Ferran suggested a one-year experiment, in an attempt to answer this question: what would happen if there was a designer working exclusively for elBulli, on the payroll? I thought it was a fantastic challenge and a career opportunity. We started this new arrangement in September 2002 with a view to the 2003 season, and extended it until 2005. After that time, we also collaborated, but on a one-off basis, and because of the friendship I had with Ferran and Albert.

How is it that we took the leap from a specific commission to such an intense collaboration? The normal thing most likely would have been to have stopped with the frozen snack plate and nothing else. I believe this continuity is due to several factors. Firstly, the way elBulli operated, which suited me. We always refer to this collaboration as 'ping-pong' because it could take two directions: they would commission me to design things, or I would pitch ideas to them. I would also say that it has something to do with the flexibility in the relationship, which meant that they might commission a plate and, once the partnership was established, at the next meeting I might propose using a candy floss machine.

There's also no doubt that it was due to my character, the fact that, with regard to other designers and artisans, I felt no need to prove myself with each item. I was of the understanding that, as far as elBulli was concerned, design was based on the needs of elBulli; it wasn't a means for me to impose my authorship. My way of understanding design is that each item has to function on its own; I have no reason to look for a style. That's why I could make things that were so different. Sometimes you look at an object and you know who designed it. That isn't my idea of design. The item had to work, and I subordinated my work to that of the restaurant. For that reason, the recipe for success was having a fixed salary, which allowed me to tackle things from all sides and not have to justify commission after commission, but to always be resolving needs.

Working for elBulli meant going to the workshop during the winter months and going up to Cala Montjoi in summer. I would normally spend two or three nights at the restaurant, and on those days I would chat with Ferran during the service. Being there on those days – those endless days – was very important for me, because working hours would start in the morning and might not finish until the end of the meal service. I had no designated space; I wasn't a

civil servant, so to speak. My work didn't involve sitting in an office. In fact, aside from Ferran, I was the one with the most freedom. When I was at the workshop, I would go out whenever I wanted to a shop or for a walk, which is the ideal way of resetting your brain, something that Ferran tends to do in all of his spaces. Everybody knows about his '*vaig i vinc*' (literally I come and I go), with those trips between elBullicarmen and elBulli workshop, or when in Cala Montjoi, between the bungalow and the restaurant.

We would sleep at elBulli, with Juli in one room (next door) and Albert Raurich, Oriol Castro and myself in the other room. My only tool was my sketch book, where I would note down all my ideas and, depending on what I saw, I would set up the next set of experiments when I returned to Barcelona. But it wasn't all work. We would sometimes head down to the nearby campsite for a few beers. Or I would sometimes have a morning swim in the sea at Cala Montjoi.

I was truly amazed at the systematic work being performed at elBulli. The huge amount of organisation with which they worked with creativity was a bit of a shock. As a designer, I was almost ashamed to see that another creative speciality worked in a much more systematic way than the one I had learnt at design school. When I was studying, when the task was to design, for instance, a wastepaper basket, three ideas might emerge; and of the three, the teacher would choose the one he felt was the best, which is the one we ended up developing. But there weren't three ideas that emerged at elBulli, but three hundred. It was then that I realised how much the structure that supports a restaurant of that calibre requires incredible organisation. Actually, when Ferran realised the importance of creativity, he gave it the same degree of organisation as he did to the other logistics of the restaurant. This was new to me. I'm not saying that there aren't other creatives in the world who don't work super-methodically. But it was unparalleled at elBulli. I would sum it up this way: to run a successful restaurant, you have to be meticulous to the extreme, and work with the same mindset.

The workshop was like that. One day they'd decide to investigate a certain product, and they would focus on multiplying ideas and tests. Or they would assign a chef exclusively to the discovery of new products. However, product design – when done on such a scale – functions much more slowly than cooking. A lot of time can pass between the designer coming up with

an idea and having it in a manufacturer's catalogue. Chefs, on the other hand, come up with an idea, test it, and if it doesn't succeed, they rule it out or correct it. In short, their cycles are much shorter.

This way of working attracted me straight away. The attitude was no longer: I have three ideas and we'll choose the best; but rather: where have I got results? What other results can this line give me? It allowed me to shift freely between techniques, between concepts, etc., which opened up a whole world of possibilities. An object didn't need to be coherent with another; what we needed was for it to be coherent with elBulli. Therefore, the resulting range is multi-colour, multi-material, multi-technique, multi-style, etc.

Moreover, hindsight also helps me to give value to what we achieved during those years. It's difficult for a designer to place value on a sheet of cellophane used to serve a lollipop; it can't be the highlight of a portfolio. But in this case, the important thing isn't the individual item, but the sum of its parts, the fact of being present at a restaurant during a service to help to underscore the gastronomic processes, in the case of objects that are used to serve food, and to create or find appliances or utensils that give rise to culinary creations.

How this book came about and how it is arranged

The origins of this book date back to 2006, when my regular collaboration with elBulli ended. At the time, I printed two copies of a selection of my sketches and I had them bound using the same format as that of my notebooks. One was a gift for Juli Soler. I've always kept the other one with me, and I'd never thought that it would be published. One day, Mireia Trius saw it and proposed having it published. And this is the result.

When it came to organising the sketches, we differentiate, first, between the concepts developed for serving food and those developed for cooking. In both groups, we make a further distinction between found and specifically designed objects.

The objects specifically designed for serving, the first chapter, correspond to the first commission. It is typical to contact a designer because you want something designed, not for them to find an object. But given the situation where we weren't able to mass produce practically anything, we soon resorted to existing things. Those objects are dealt with in the second chapter. In the third chapter, we look at objects found in other areas, but which were suited for use in a kitchen, in

other words, to produce culinary creations. Later, in the fourth chapter, are the utensils and appliances designed for cooking. This field emerged quite coincidentally. When Albert discovered spherification, it became necessary to invent the caviar maker in order to make lots of spherical melon droplets at the same time. The final chapter is a compilation of ideas, sketches and drawings – not always associated with cuisine – that were found in the same notebooks.

This book is therefore the fruit of hundreds of ideas that our dynamic at elBulli filtered out, and which I have also selected in order to make it possible to understand what such a rewarding interdisciplinary collaboration represented for me, and I hope readers find it interesting.

Specifically designed objects for serving

This chapter corresponds to the first commission I was given by Albert Adrià, and was in response to a brilliant stroke of inspiration: taking advantage of the fact that my studio was very near to the elBulli workshop, instead of buying a special plate, they commissioned a designer to come up with one. On the following pages I've arranged the catalogue of objects according to their materiality and/or the technique used to produce them.

Custom slate

Vacuum bags as a food holder

Custom packaging

Extruded plastic cut to measure

Unmoulded blown glass

Transmaterialisation

Silversmithing techniques

Metal mesh

Thermoformed glass

Paper tableware

Screen-printed glass

Mass stamping

Slate platters

The slate platters were a response to the first request I received from Ferran: a holder for serving frozen snacks. Some of these items were actually among the first I came up with for the restaurant. Starting with this requirement, I began to research, and I found out that slate was a material with a high heat storage coefficient. In other words, if chilled, it stays cold for a long time. The same thing happens with heat.

What was missing was a supplier with whom we could work comfortably. We found one in Cardedeu, halfway between Barcelona and Cala Montjoi. The slate was supplied by Xavier Gelabert, who sent them directly to the stonecutter Gerard Alejandro, who was responsible for shaping the items. This collaboration offered us a wide range of possibilities.

It was an extremely suitable material to work with because it could be made into ten platters, and then another ten. Because they weren't made on an industrial scale, we could ask tradesmen who turned slate into flooring to cut the pieces to measure and make grooves, holes, etc.

Each platter was actually adapted to the preparation that had been previously created with this in mind. For example,

the size of the groove on one of our first platters, which was used to serve a frozen pastille, was dictated by the dimensions of the silicone mould used to make the pastille.

There were slates with a number of different grooves, with one hole, two holes, three, four, which allowed tables with different numbers of customers to be served. There were also slates that could hold a bowl, or slates without either grooves or holes, which were used as dishes for snacks. The use of slates became very popular later, and you can still see them today in many restaurants.

Once I had spent long periods of time in the restaurant later on, I became aware of one major problem with these designs, their weight. The waiting staff would carry huge trays covered with slates. Just seeing them walking down the corridor to the dining room, burdened down with this weight, I could feel my back hurting...

Specifically designed objects for serving

Slate platter
2 holes

Slate platter
3 holes

Slate platter
4 holes

Slate platter
16 x 12 cm

Slate platter
20 x 9 cm

Slate platter
5 grooves

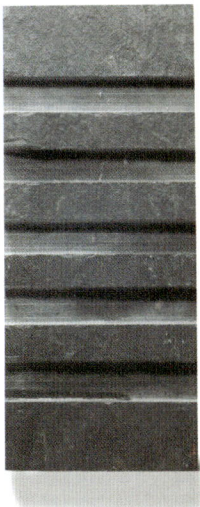

Slate platter
1 groove

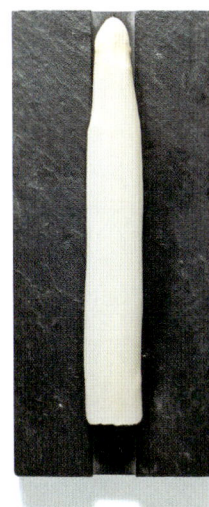

Slate platter
10 x 10 cm

Slate platter
20 x 20 cm

Slate platter
10 x 10 cm honed

Holder for frozen snacks

🏭. Idea for an industrial version

This focused on creating plugs to fit
into the four corners of the slate platters,
so that they could be stacked.

- cristal?
- pelustería.

logo.

h.le te.

plato

personalizable para restaurantes y hoteles.

clic.

apilable para
- venta
- almacenamiento
- colocación del conjel.

Cold-hot bag

I've already mentioned that the first commission I received from elBulli was a holder that allowed frozen snacks to be served. A frozen snack can be an incredible thing, but if it was served on any plate, it was highly likely that its structure wouldn't cope with having to travel the twenty metres between the kitchen and dining room.

So I looked for a solution to enable the preparation to stay chilled. One of them was the typical gel pack that is sold in pharmacies, which can keep things cold or hot for a long time. So I bought one, opened it and put the gel into vacuum bags. I then had the word 'elBullisnack' screen-printed onto it and we used it as a holder for frozen preparations.

Cone with label

This is a double concept: the cone, inspired by the paper cones used to serve churros and the accompanying label. The fun we had with the cone was when making it very small. It was used to serve frozen watermelon pellets, known as *shot* and later for hazelnut nitro-shot, which was served with a sprinkling of roasted hazelnut skin powder.

As far as the label goes, it had occurred to me that brands were becoming increasingly visible on the food served at certain establishments, for instance fast-food restaurants, so I proposed to mimic the practice with irony.

Sniff

Sniff was a plastic tube filled with porcini mushroom jelly that was sucked, as if through a straw. The idea behind it was to imitate the action of sucking the marrow from a bone, which made this a sort of artificial marrow bone.

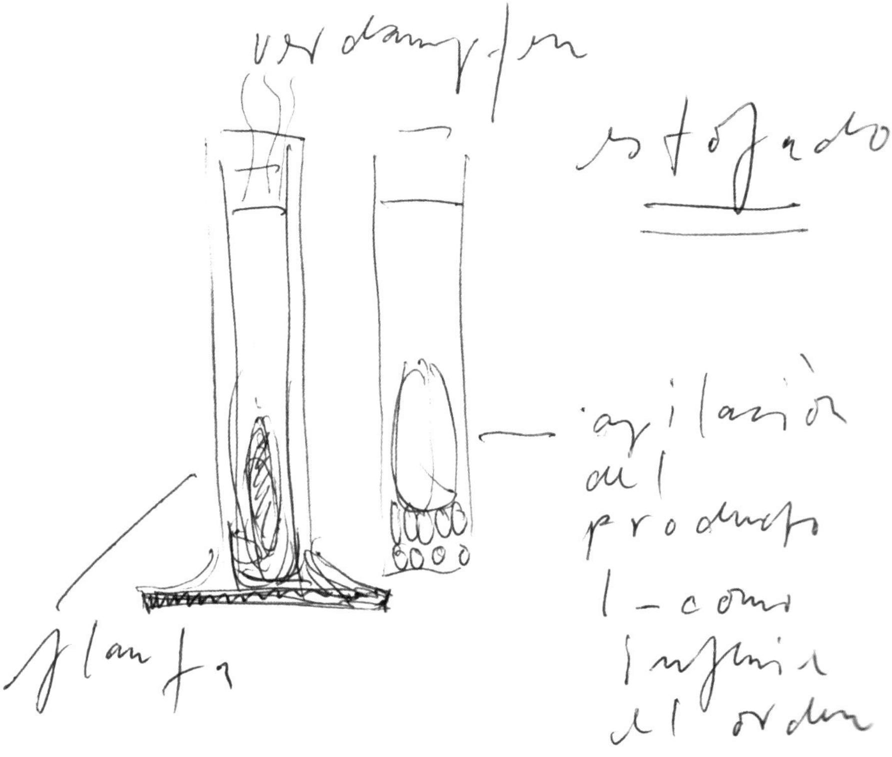

verdampfen

estofado

planta

agilación
del
producto
l — como
imagen
del orden

Capillary skewer

⬛.. Idea for an industrial version

This idea is very similar to that of the pipette-skewer, although based on the principle of capillary action, thanks to which the sauce stays inside the skewer.

It would require the extrusion of a stick perforated with a lot of holes. When dipped into a very runny sauce, capillary action would cause the sauce to rise, and the skewer could then be inserted into a product. The effect would be the same as that of the pipette: eating a solid preparation and then sucking the sauce.

Once again, production was found to be unfeasible, given that thousands of metres of tubing would be required, although there was always the possibility of taking the project to industrial level for commercial exploitation.

*

— Preis
trocknet
schneller

Trocknen;

— oberflächen-
spannung
des
inhalts

— querschnitt

— länge /
querschnitt
verhält
niss.

* mehrere
Kanäle

1. [sketch] → 2. [sketch]   3. [sketch] — = langsamte
durch
trocknen !

Suction cups for skewers and sniffs

⚙. Idea for an industrial version

This suction cup was meant to be a holder that would allow the skewers and sniffs to be served at the table. It would also serve as the bottom plug for the sniffs when it came to filling them.

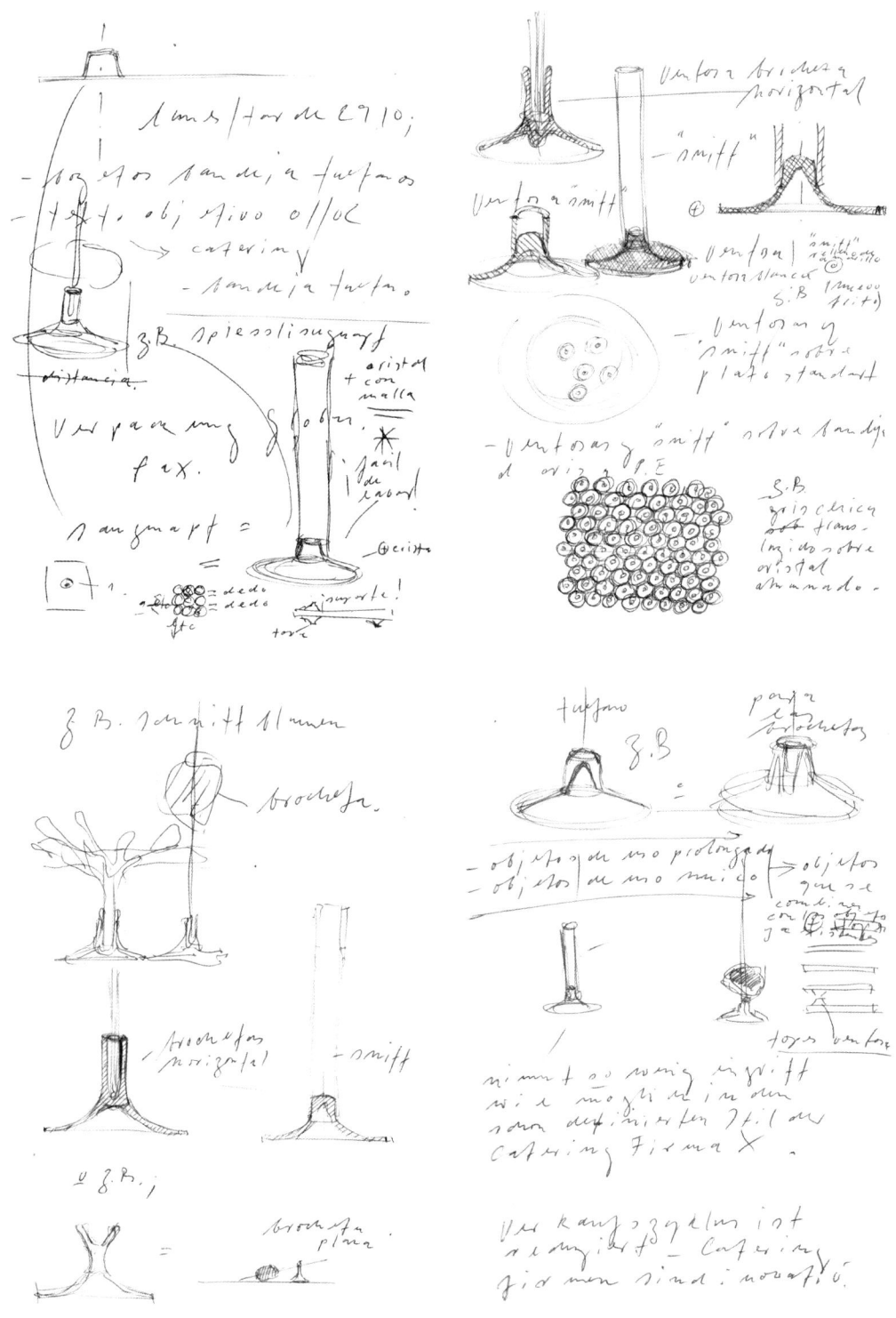

Bowls

The limitation of not being able to mass produce items meant that we couldn't make moulds for this purpose. We soon discovered that there were artisan glass blowers working at Pueblo Español and we proposed a collaboration. What they did was to blow reasonably large balls that would later be cut in different ways. From them we obtained 'eggs' in different sizes.

One of the consequences of working without a mould was, logically, that each piece would be slightly different. The following pages show several of these glass objects, such as the one used to serve the first carrot air, a 'giant' but extremely light portion that was served to each diner. Or the egg which held a spoon with a spherical pea raviolo. However, most were generic and weren't used for any particular preparation.

We also came to make a 'hovering plate', a glass egg which was covered with cling film. After trimming with a paper cutter and topping with a preparation, it gave the impression of being a solid piece of glass, or more importantly, that the food was suspended in the air. Other glass eggs were the vertical egg and the forerunner to the bowl containing a glove, the so-called 'farewell bowl', the final version of which was made out of metal.

Air bowl

Spoon bowl

Snack bowl S
Snack bowl M
Snack bowl L

Vertical egg bowl
Hovering bowl

Glass bowls

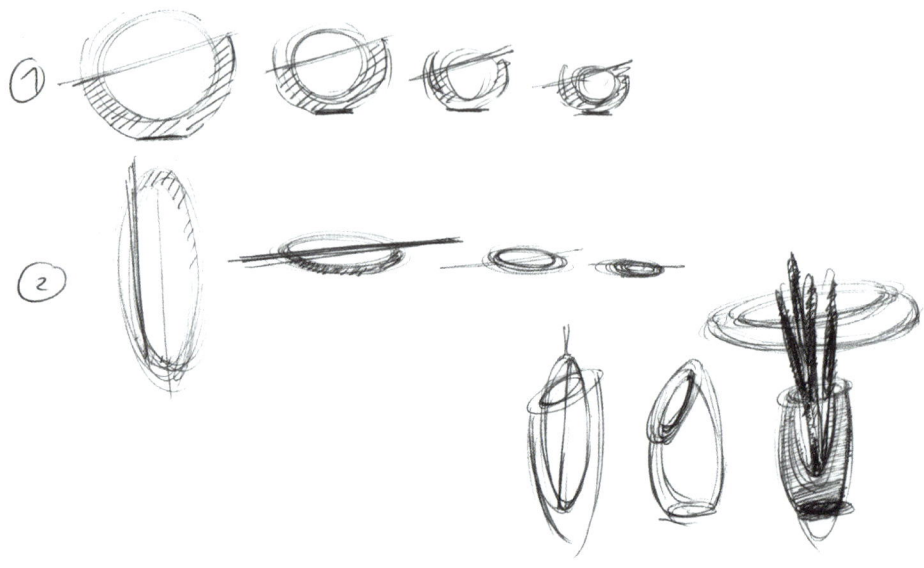

Glove bowl

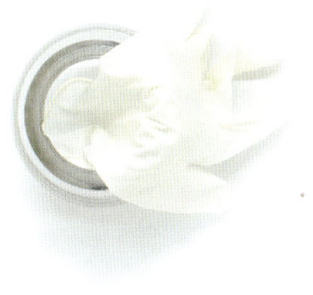

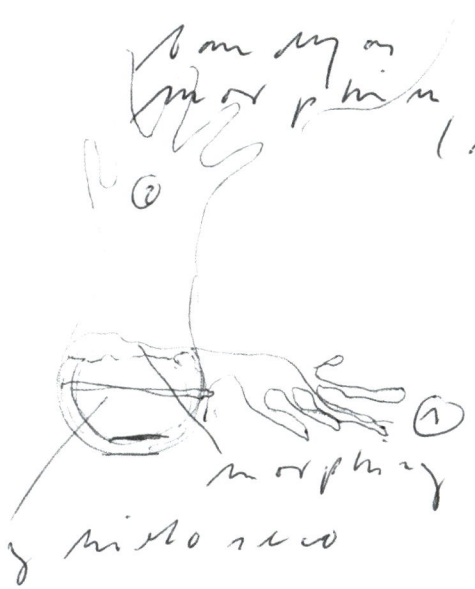

Glass bowls

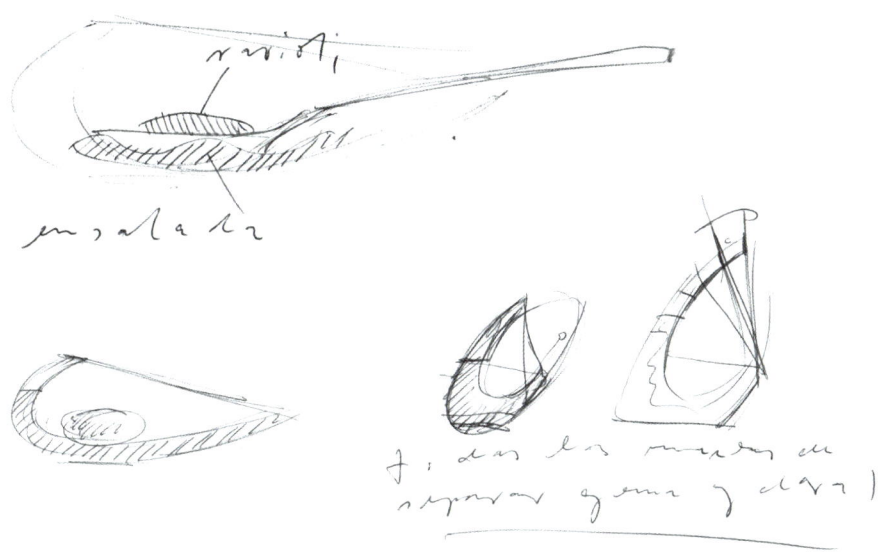

Transmaterialisation

There is a technique in the world of jewellery-making known as lost wax casting, which consists of making a piece in wax, encasing it in plaster and pouring a molten metal into the mould. This melts the wax to leave a space with the exact shape of the object. Instead of wax, the process can also be done with any material that melts without leaving any residue.

In collaboration with the jeweller Jaime Díaz, we bought silver and encased everyday plastic objects in the plaster, for the purpose of turning them into silver objects. By doing this, we made a typical ice-cream spoon, a coffee stirrer/spoon, and a medicine spoon.

The ice-cream spoon was extremely successful, to the point where, together with the caviar tin, it was one of the items to 'vanish' the most easily. While eating an ice cream is fantastic in itself, eating it at elBulli with a classic spoon, but made of silver, was a stroke of magic.

When making the coffee spoon, I found that the original plastic stirrer was so thin that its 'transmaterialisation' in silver could bend easily. I solved this problem by gluing the two flat sides of the stirrers together, resulting in the finished spoon having relief on both sides.

The medicine spoon took the idea of having control over what is served in a preparation to the extreme, and by including the milligram markings, it conveyed the precision that had always been sought at elBulli.

Ice-cream spoon

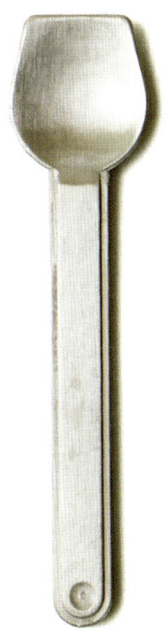

Coffee spoon

Medicine spoon

Other possible transmaterialised cutlery

Another important point was that the objects could be melted down again, in theory, to recover the silver should we, at some other time, decide to turn it into something else.

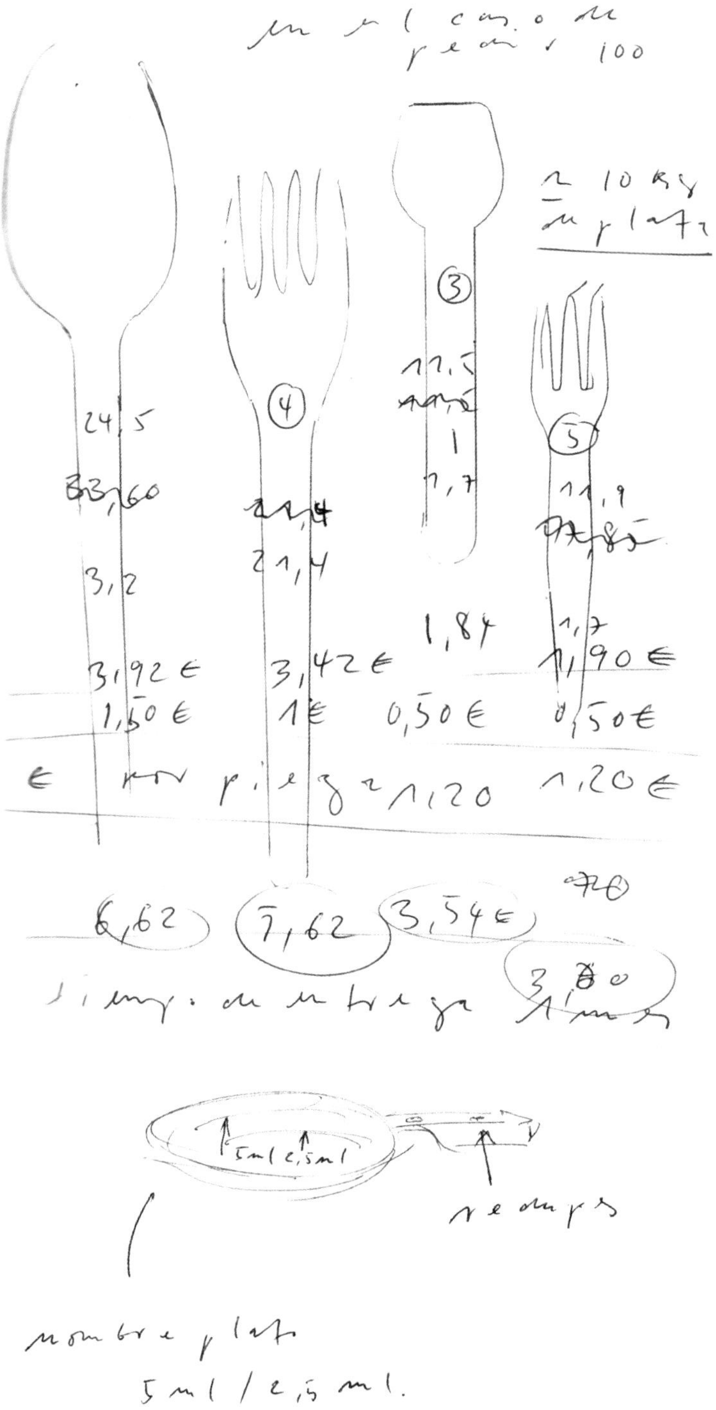

un ~ l cas o de
pe... 100

~ 10 kg
~p lat.

③

④ ⑤

24,5

33,60

3,2

11,5

1

7,7

11,9

21,4

21,4

1,84

1,7

3,92 €   3,42 €   1,90 €

1,50 €   1 €   0,50 €   0,50 €

€   ... pi e g a 1,20   1,20 €

6,62   7,62   3,54 €   72

3,80

d i ... de ... tre ga

nombre plato
5 ml / 2,5 ml.

5 ml / 2,5 ml

recamps

Concentrate spoon

When we began to work on the FACES collection, the goldsmiths Cunill Orfebres gave me easy access to their facilities, which allowed me to do a lot of things using the techniques of the trade. In this case, it was a spoon without the typical bowl. The handle was that of a spoon, but the end was flat instead of concave. I had the word CONCENTRADO (concentrate) engraved along the handle, and where the final O should have been, a drop of tarragon concentrate was placed.

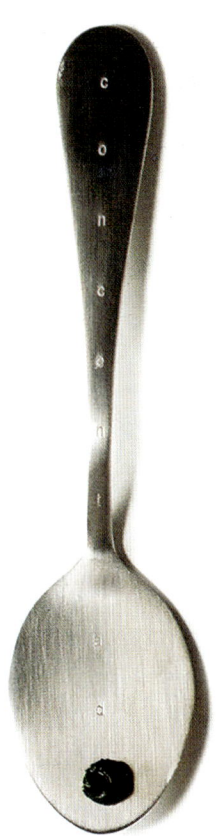

Fragrance spoon

When it came to the concepts associated with the perception of smell, we came up with an idea: to make a spoon that would allow one thing to be eaten while smelling something different. At one point, at the elBulli workshop, I witnessed the creation of the most fantastic prototype I'd ever seen. Oriol Castro went out into the courtyard, picked an orange flower and taped it to a conventional spoon. Just seeing this, we knew that it would work. Eating something and smelling something else. It was a kind of mental fruit salad!

When it came to creating the final design, I put forward two solutions: the first was a spoon with a tubular handle, which allowed a herb or flower to be placed inside the handle.

Soup fragrance spoon

The second solution, which was larger,
consisted of a handle with a notch to allow
a fragrant item to be inserted.

Fragrance spoon

⌘.. Idea for an industrial version

These are some of the sketches for the fragrance spoon, with different solutions, once we saw how interesting it could be to eat the contents of the spoon while smelling a herb, a flower or something else.

For instance, the handle could be bent to work like a pair of tweezers. Or a tube could be created to allow a fragrance to be released continuously. Another version came with a cylindrical hole in the handle where fragrant paper could be inserted.

I also thought of having a thread coming out with which things of different diameters could be rolled up. I always felt the thread should be red. The German for 'red thread' is *roter Faden*, which also means 'guiding thread'. In fact, in the first years of life in Barcelona, I always carried a spool of red thread in my pocket, which was my guiding thread.

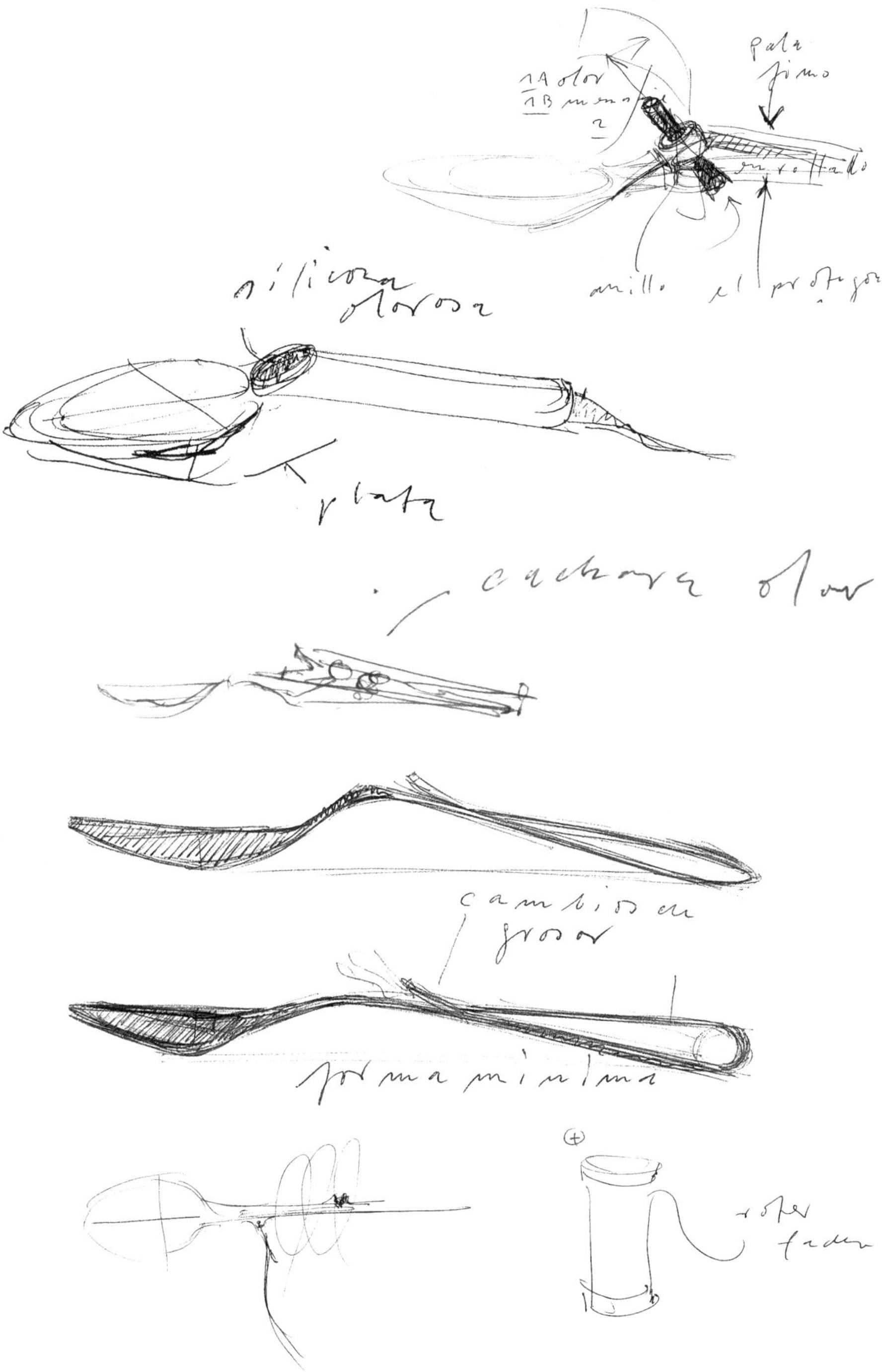

↑A olor
↑B menos
2

pala
firmo

anillo   el proteger

silicona
olorosa

plata

cuchara olor

cambio en
grosor

forma minima

⊕

rober
frder

Butter knife

Before devoting myself to design as a career, I worked as a jeweller for a couple of years, which at the time gave me an understanding of working with metal. So I made this knife, like the rest of the series – the nigiri spatula and nitro-dragon spatula – out of silver-plated brass.

This knife was designed as a set with the butter dish to serve smoked coconut butter. Given that the preparation was used as a butter, the knife was laser-engraved with the pictogram used at elBulli for dairy prod- ucts.

Nigiri spatula

This spatula, which was laser-engraved with a tongue, was derived from the design of a tongue depressor. It was used to allow different proportions of a preparation to be served on different surfaces of small size. The tongue spatula was used in 2004 to serve a nigiri.

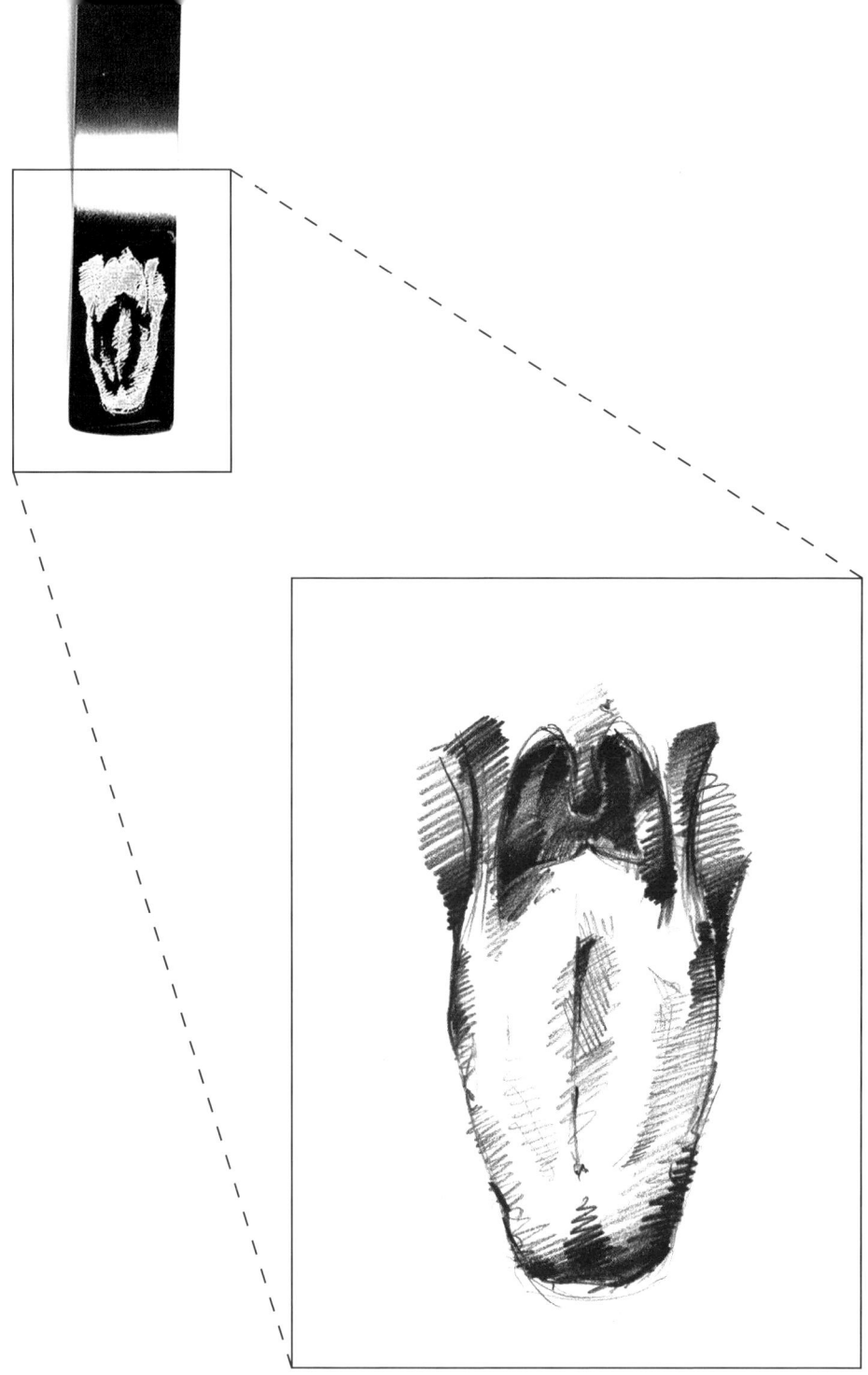

Original drawing by Marta Méndez Blaya

Nitro-dragon spatula

This spatula was used in 2004 to serve the liquorice nitro-dragon, a preparation akin to a foam – which was given the name of Texlavazza at elBulli – that was subsequently dipped in liquid nitrogen. Because of its chemical composition, liquorice retains a lot of steam when frozen, which meant that when placed in the mouth, it would release what appeared to be a thick puff of smoke, as if the diner were a dragon.

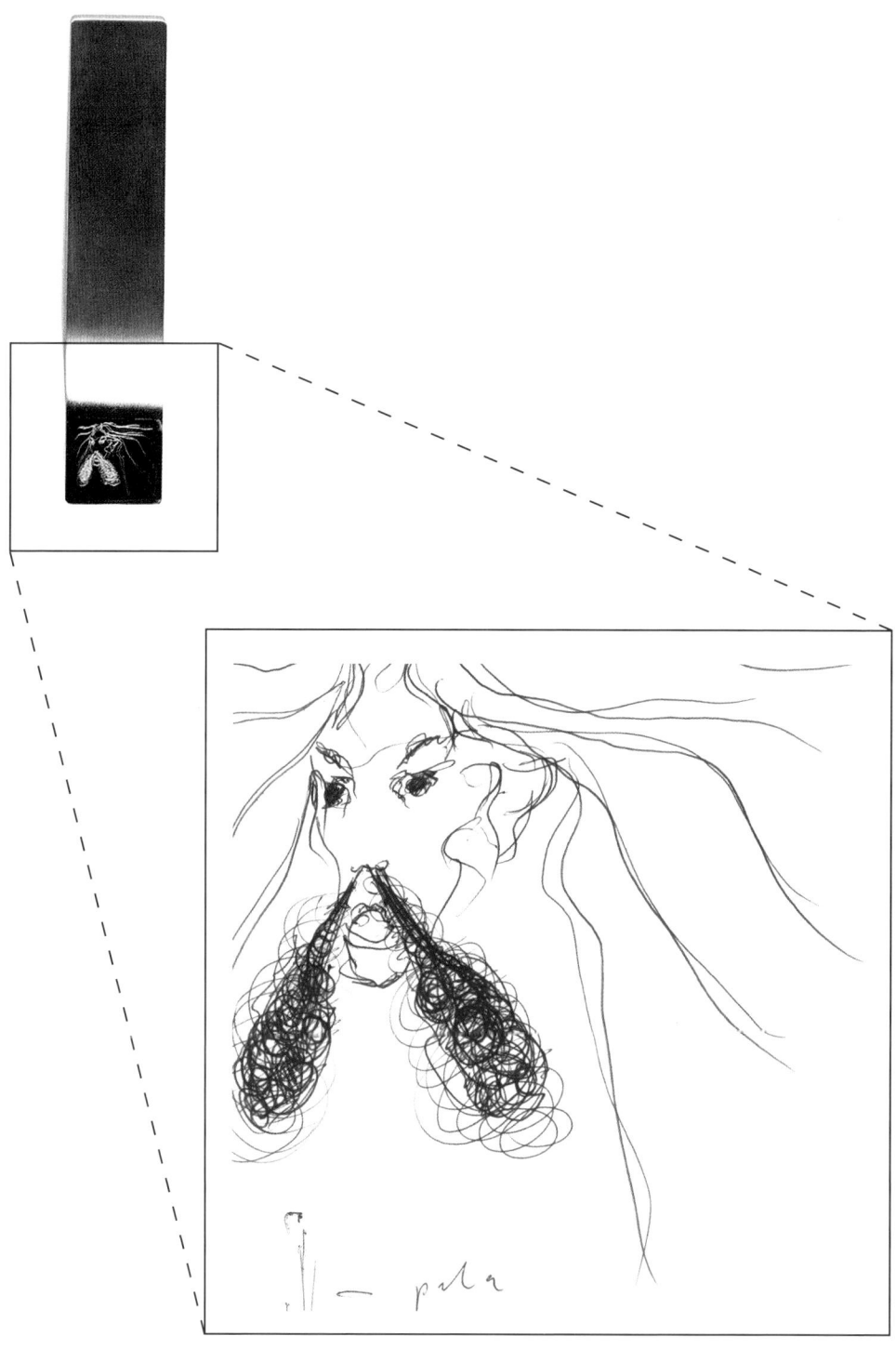

Butter dish

In this case, the idea was to play with the fact that the butter is whitish, and to make a butter dish out of a nylon cube, into which a hole was drilled and filled with coconut butter.

Meringue box

These silver-plated brass 'seats',
each of which I made by hand,
were the containers used to serve
individual meringues to each diner.

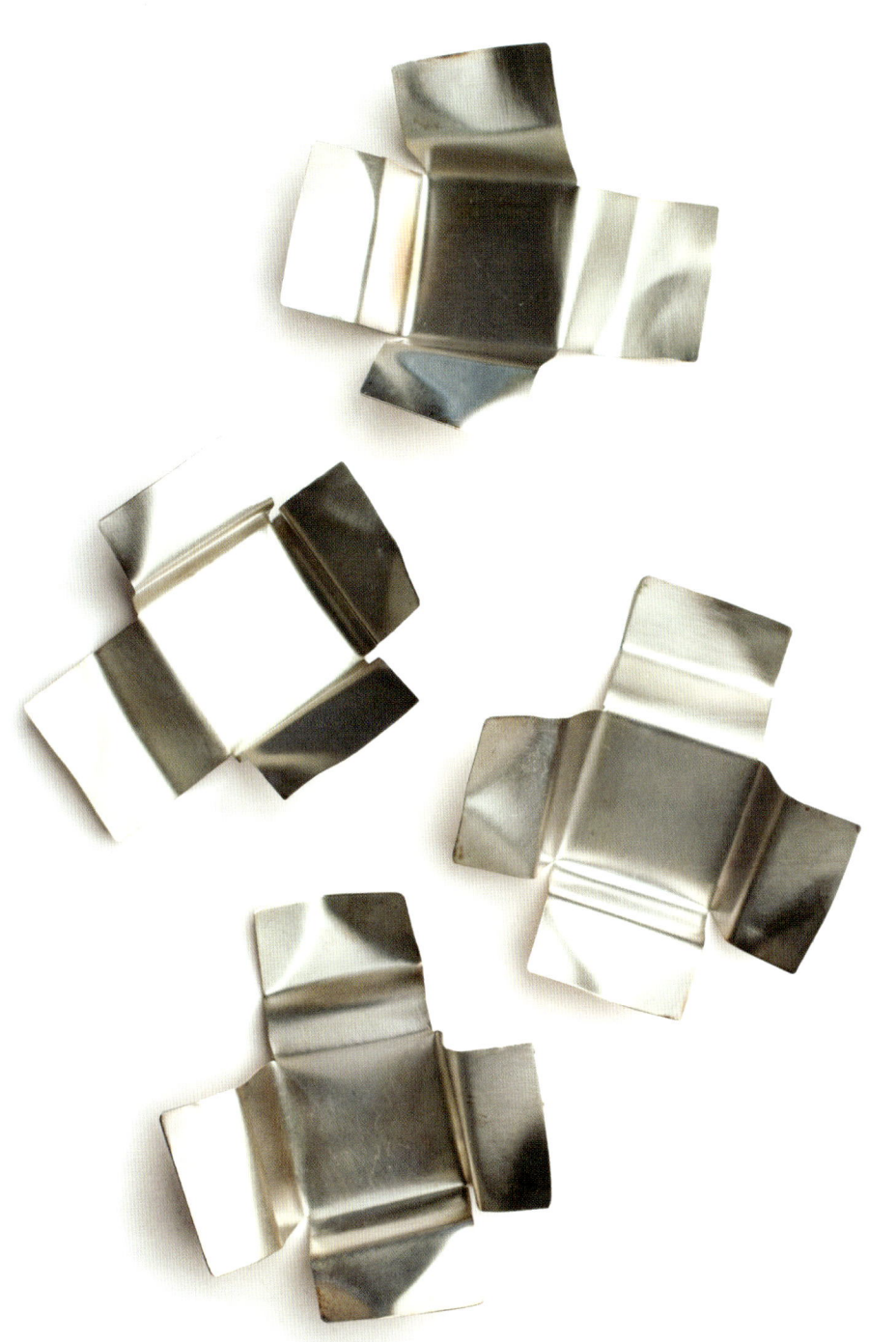

Farewell bowl

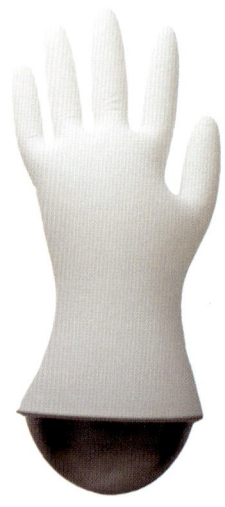

This is the definitive version of a design that was initially conceived using a glass bowl. The glove that covered the bowl would sway when carried by the waiter, like a hand waving goodbye. For this to happen, the bowl had to be completely hemispherical, i.e. without a flat base. When the glove was removed, the bowl inside held small marshmallows. Once the contents had been eaten, the diner could see a hand engraved inside the bowl, a reference to shaking the hands of the people who had shared a few hours of their time with us.

Farewell bowl

Sketch for the design of the bowl covered by a glove and which represented saying farewell to customers. The design was first made into a glass bowl, later replaced by the definitive version in metal.

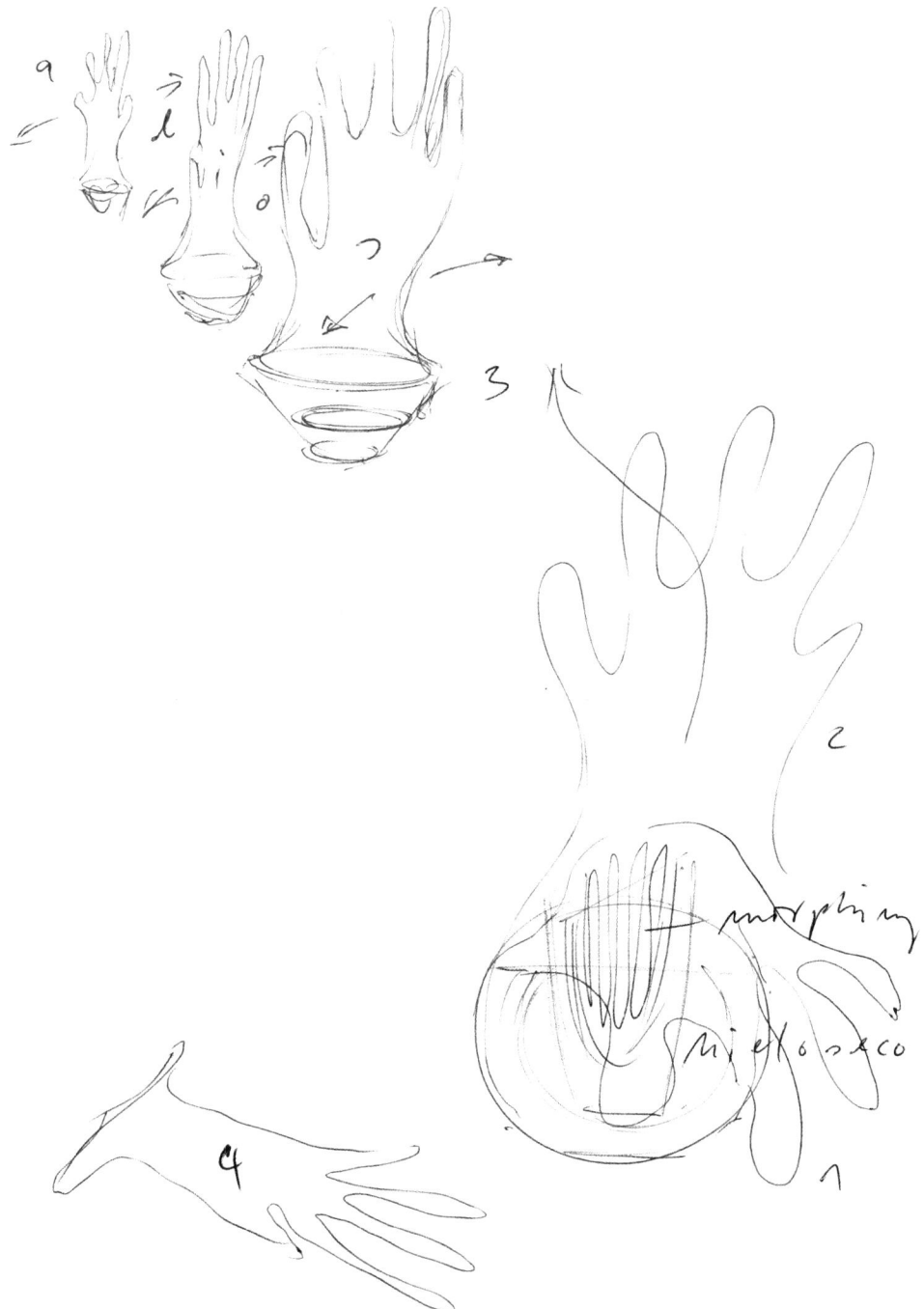

Graphic design for the farewell bowl

Following on with the icon of the glove as a farewell, at a given moment, I'd given thought to printing a few fingerprints on it, in order to have a view from close up (the fingerprint) and from afar (the hand) on the same plane. Finally, this project did not come to fruition in this way, given that we resorted to another design for the graphic on the second version of the farewell bowl.

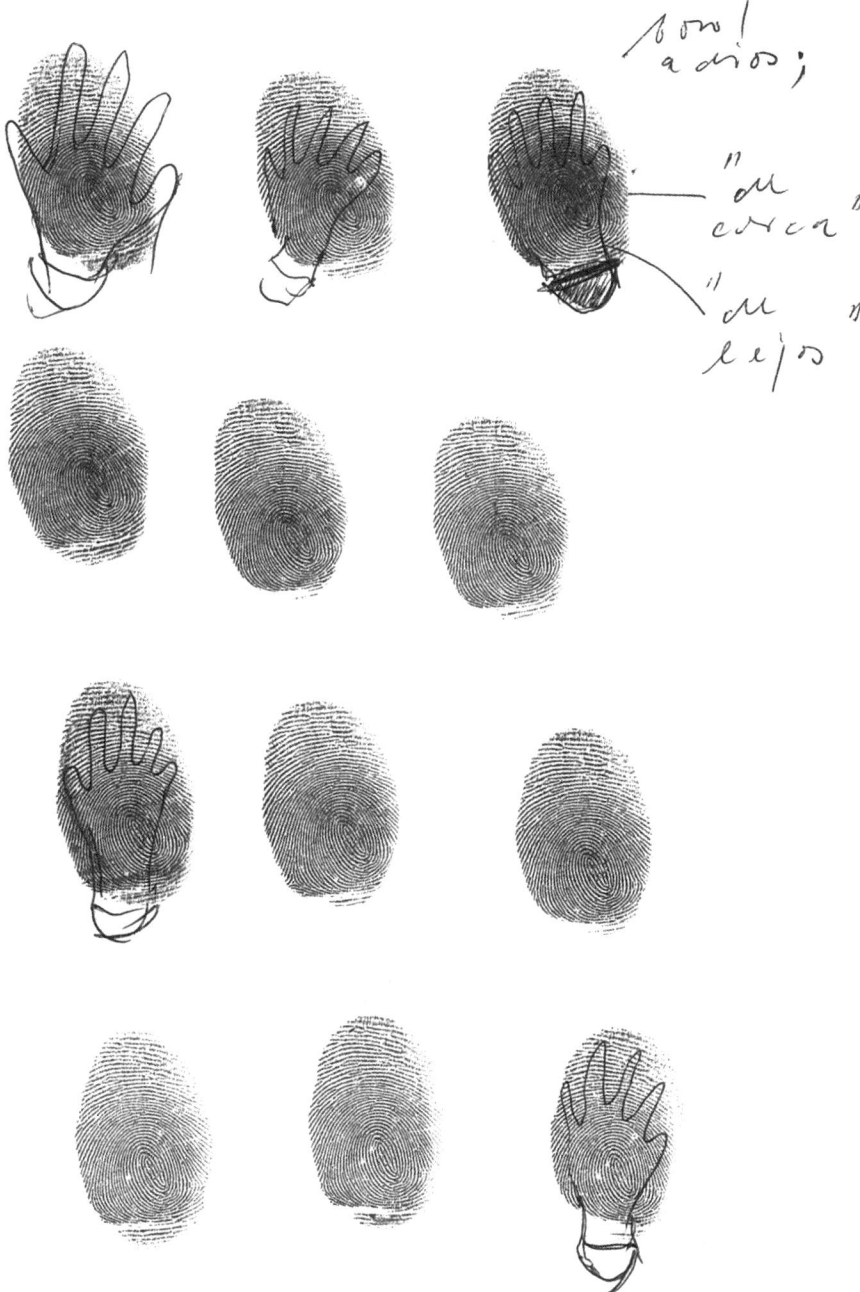

bon!
adiós;

"de
cerca"

"de
lejos"

Flower pot

This silver-plated brass flower pot could be used to plant herbs, but also hold twigs that would later be decorated with balls of candy floss.

Bread platter and paper with flour pictogram stamp

This platter, which held the air-baguette, was made of corrugated and perforated sheet metal which we pressed at Cunill. The platter is a reference to the trays used by bakeries for baking baguettes.

Baroque platters

The rationale behind the baroque platters was to utilise the moulds used by Cunill to make platters, frames and other items. Our contribution was to leave the excess before trimming, which created a contrast between the refinement of the centre, classical in style, and the more contemporary lines marked by the exterior.

The moulds already existed, making it possible to stamp the small quantities that interested us. We produced several versions, in silver-plated and even gold-plated brass.

Baroque platters

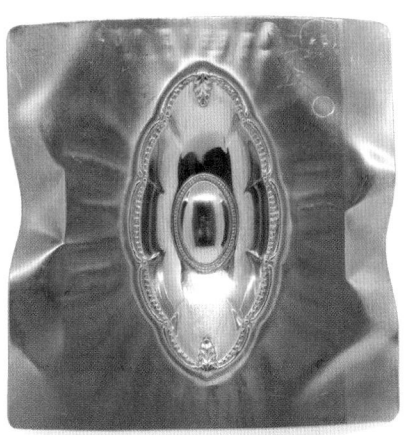
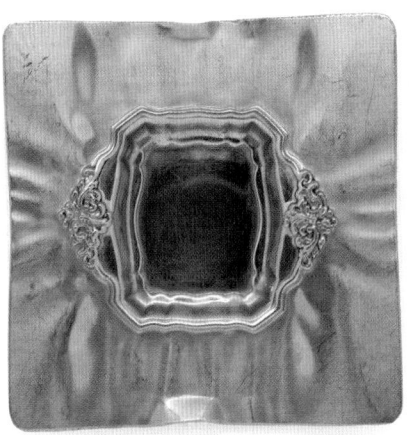
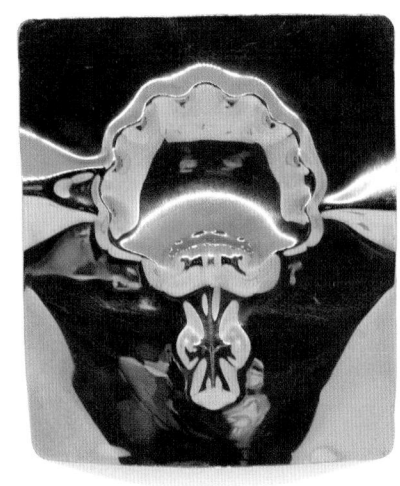

Gold-plated baroque platters

These platters were a part of the baroque tableware series, although in this case they were distinguished by the gold plating, which gave them an even more classical patina. They were widely used because they could serve all sorts of snacks and morphings (snacks that bridge the change from salty to sweet) that could be eaten directly with the fingers.

Gold-plated punnet

This punnet, made in gold-plated sheet metal, was a reference to plastic punnets.

Long zigzag platter

We gave the name 'zigzag' to this entire family of platters because it's the word used in Spain for the typical paper napkins found in the dispensers used in bars, which often end up crumpled next to the plate. Just like the baroque platters, they were used to serve all kinds of dry snacks and morphings, with the exception of the odd model designed to hold spoons.

A selection of these platters was later commercialised under the FACES label.

Glossy zigzag platter
Matt zigzag bowl platter

Zigzag platter for medicine spoons

Zigzag platters

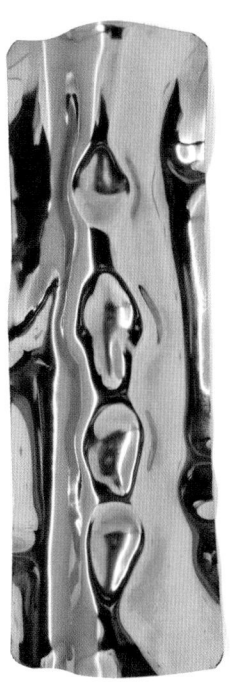

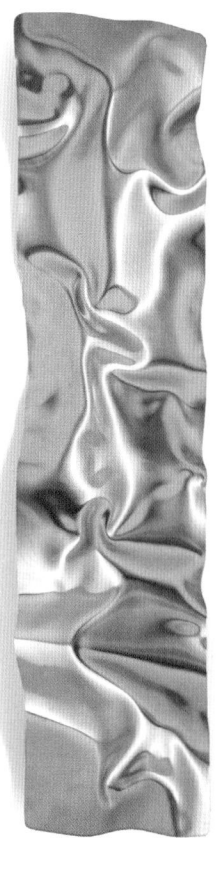

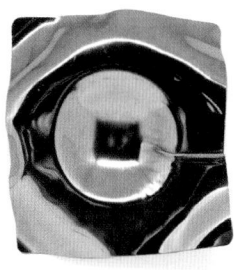

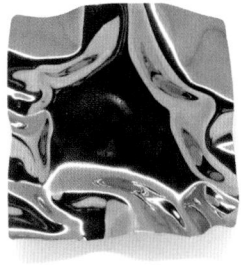

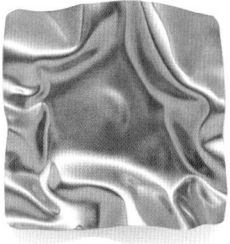

Gold-plated zigzag platters

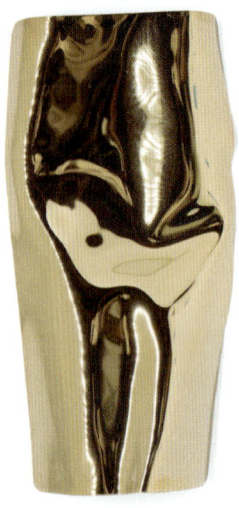

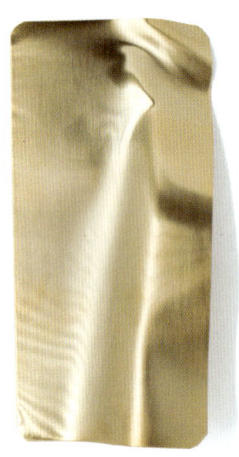

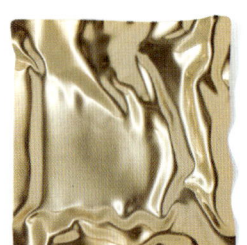

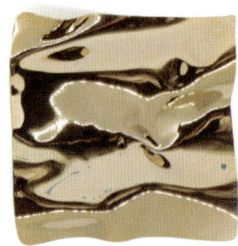

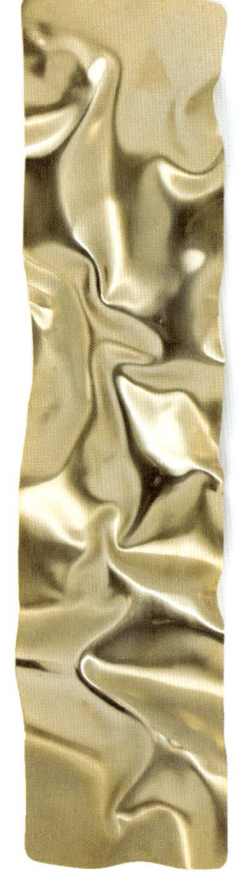

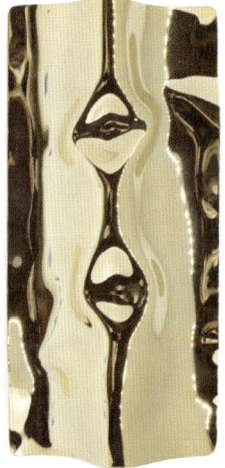

'Memoformed' platters

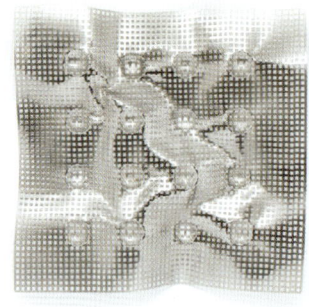

This set of stainless steel tableware was created using a mould consisting of a modular system with two plates and a series of pistons. Depending on how we positioned the pistons, the result was one type of tableware or another. In other words, depending on how each one of the pistons (in this case sixteen) was positioned, a specific design was created.

Platter made using the memoforming technique, in this case applied to previously perforated sheets of metal.

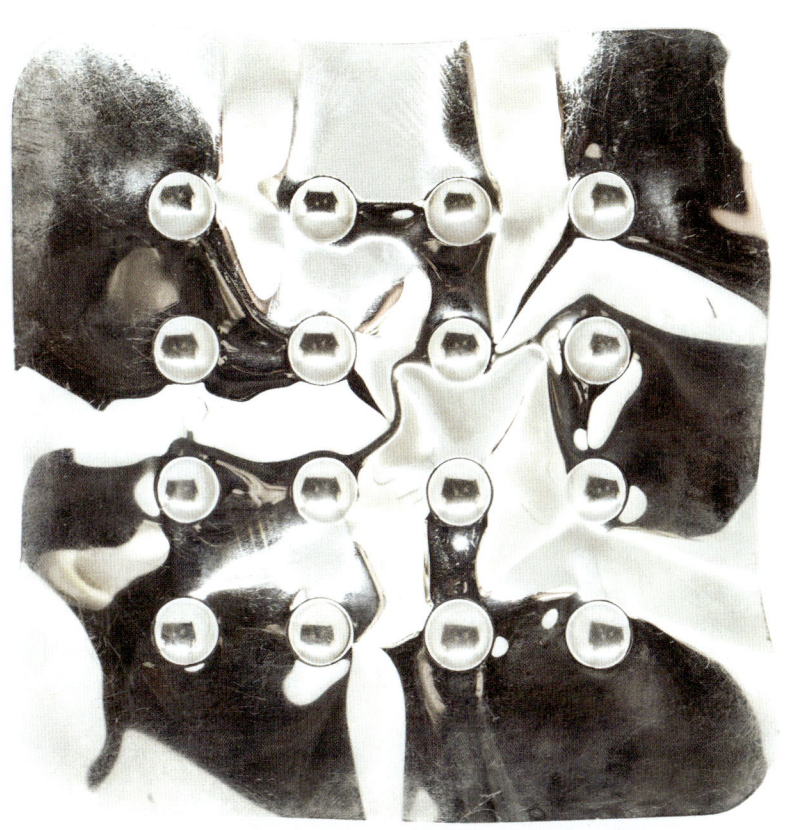

'Memoformed' tableware

Design of the mould for the memoformed
tableware.

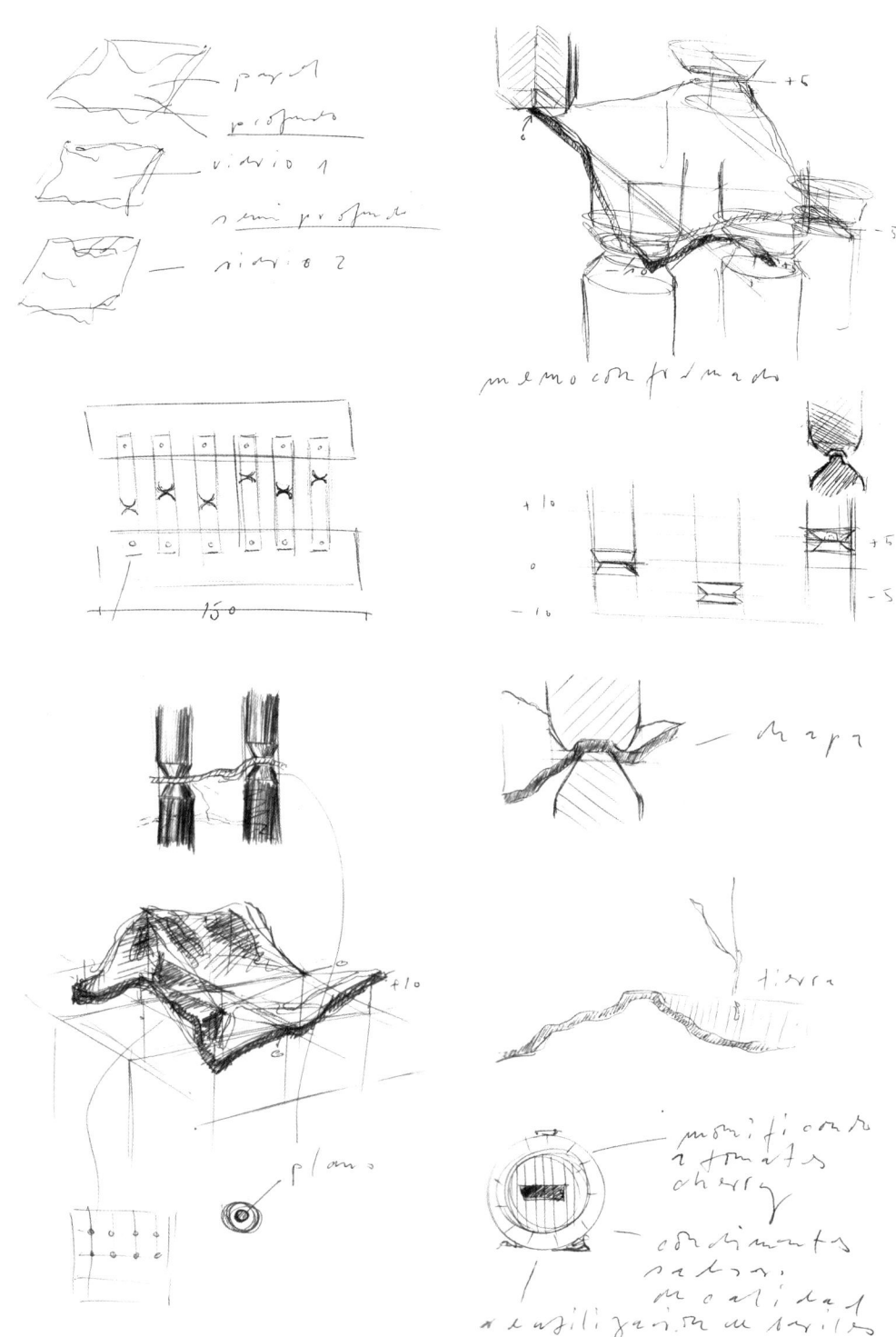

Mesh platters

Here's another example of the problems we encountered by the fact that we needed small numbers of each item. At times, the kitchen would require three of one type of plate, four types of holders, etc., and there are few techniques available that enable the production of short runs.

One arose when working with stainless steel mesh. This material is very suitable for serving food in terms of hygiene, and it can also be moulded by hand. The only problem I had to resolve was that the edge was quite sharp, which forced me to fold it over. In this way, once a part of the mesh was folded, it was no longer dangerous and could be given the desired shape. At that time there were two guys on a work placement, Jaume and Henrik, who worked to make the set and ended up with their fingers pricked and covered in plasters.

This design was made up very spontaneously, a good example of 'ping-pong' between design and cuisine. if a certain shape was needed? It was produced on the spot, and if it worked, it was reproduced.

Another model with folds resembled a crumpled cloth napkin. One smaller model was made using a mould, and it served to hold the spoon containing the tarragon concentrate. The mould was made of resin and the pressing was done at Cunill, allowing each piece to be exactly the same.

Mesh platter with two compartments

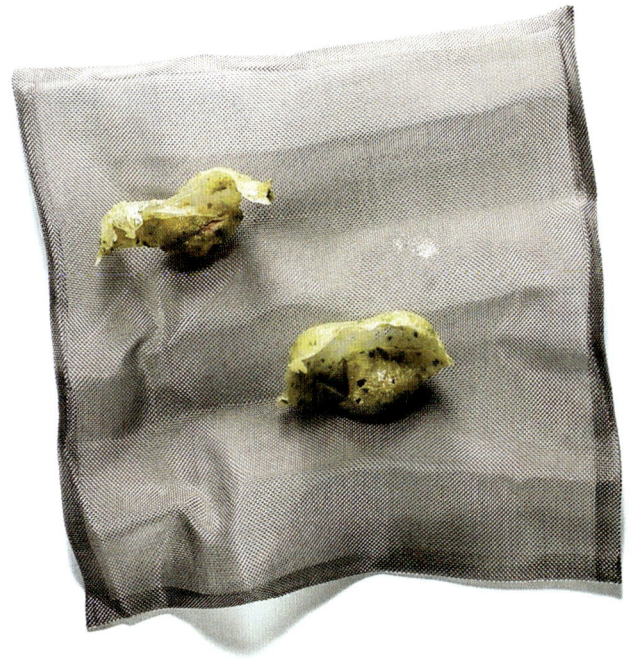

Mesh platter

Mesh platter for spoon

Mesh platters

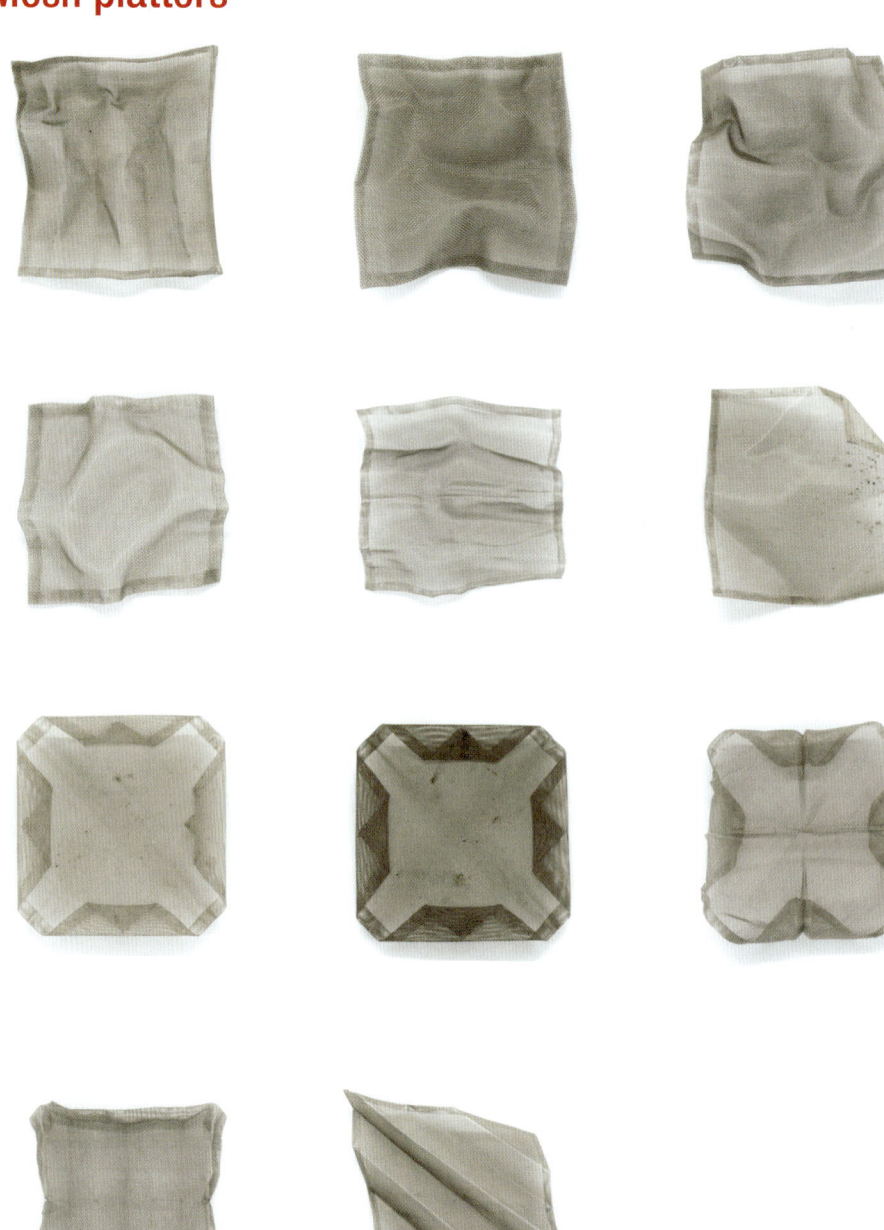

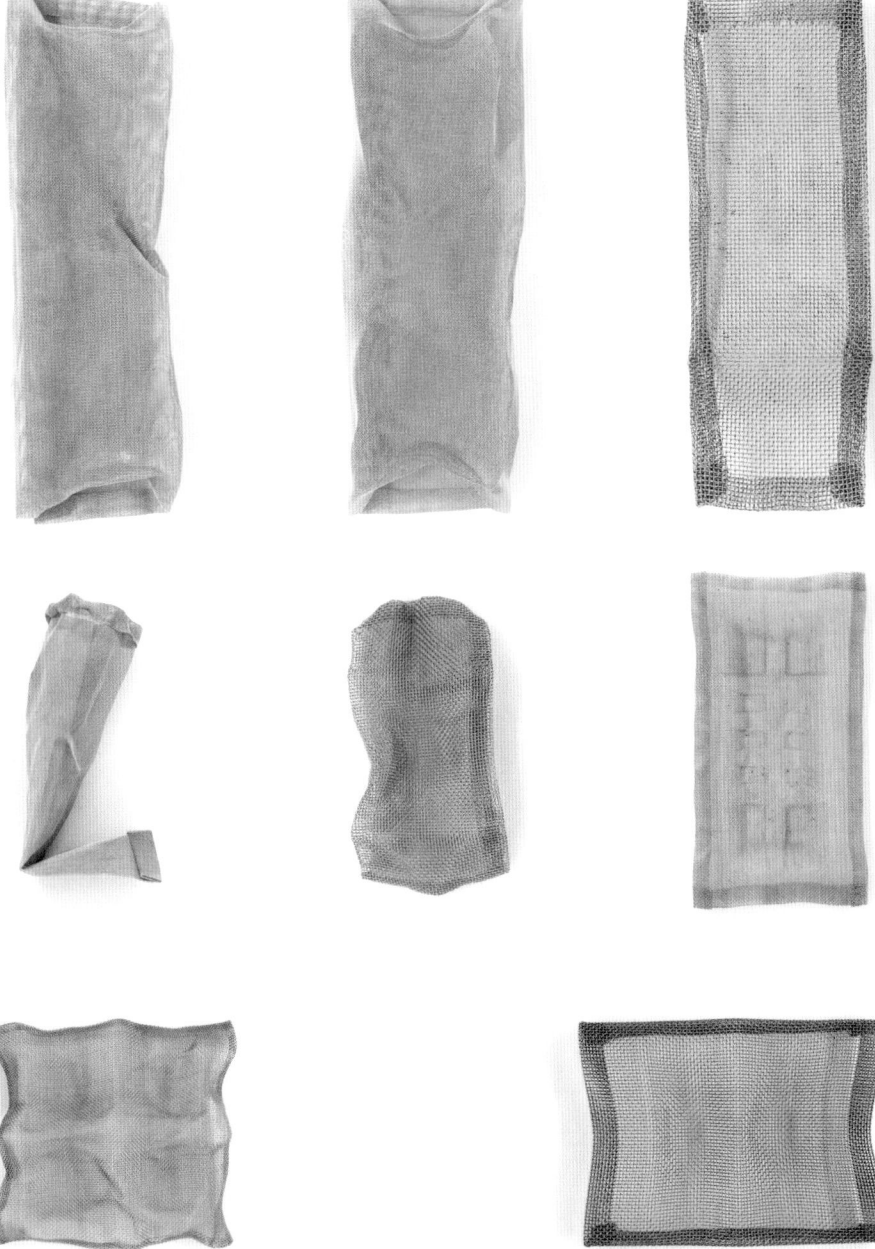

Glass platters

The glass thermoforming process allowed us to make limited numbers of each platter. This process starts with a flat glass sheet that is placed over a mould before heat is applied. The glass then adapts to the mould, which actually tends to be very economical.

The first platters used were those that the Luesma & Vega glass studio already had. However, they served me as a template for all the metal platters we made together with Cunill. We were also able to make very simple moulds, for example, by perforating refractory bricks with a drill or by cutting with a water jet, or even by placing the glass over very simple existing objects, such as stones found in Cala Montjoi.

This type of manufacturing became a goldmine, allowing us to produce short runs of tableware for the restaurant industry in general. Hence the large number of sketches aimed at defining moulds and systems for working with this process.

Glass zigzag platter

Glass bowl platter

Glass platter for spoon

Glass platters

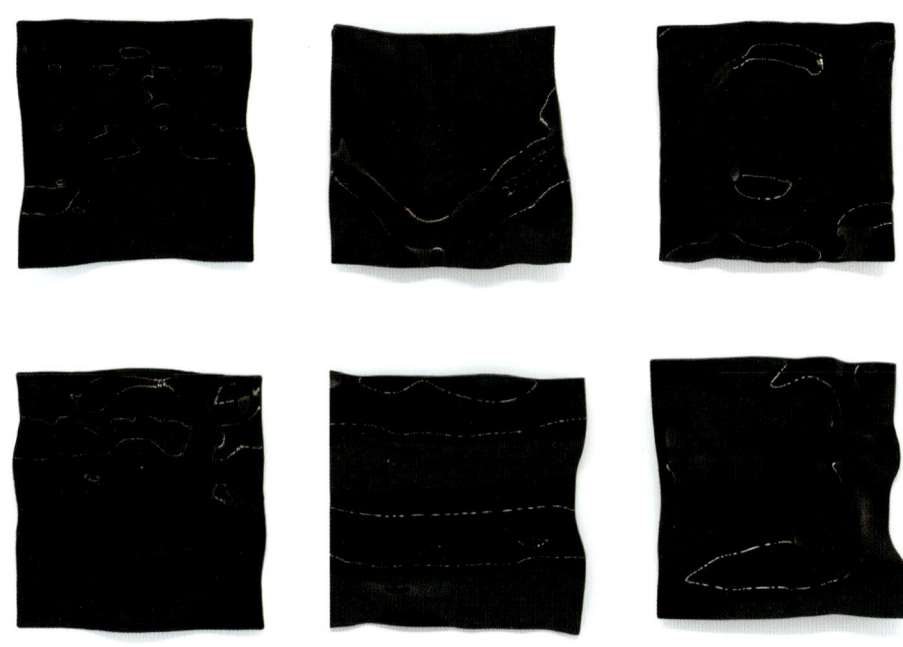

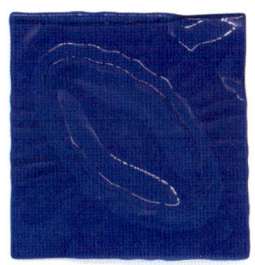

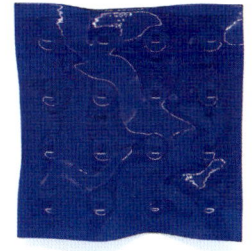

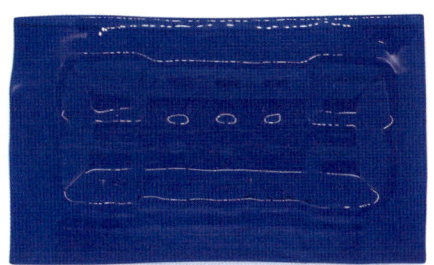

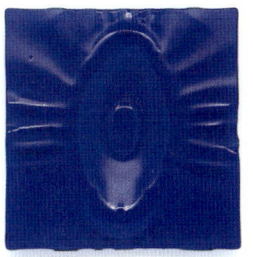

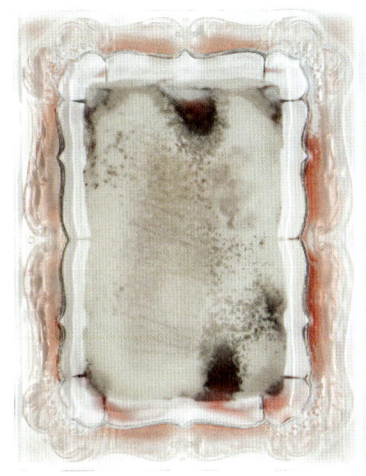

Sketches for glass platters

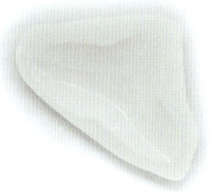

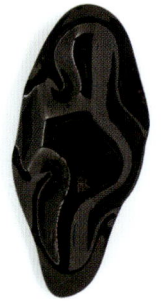

The glass thermoforming process is undoubtedly the optimum technology for producing small runs; in fact, it is commonly used today. At the time, I thought up a lot of designs based on the possibilities of these limited runs. Today I continue to think that this technique offers huge opportunities to be explored.

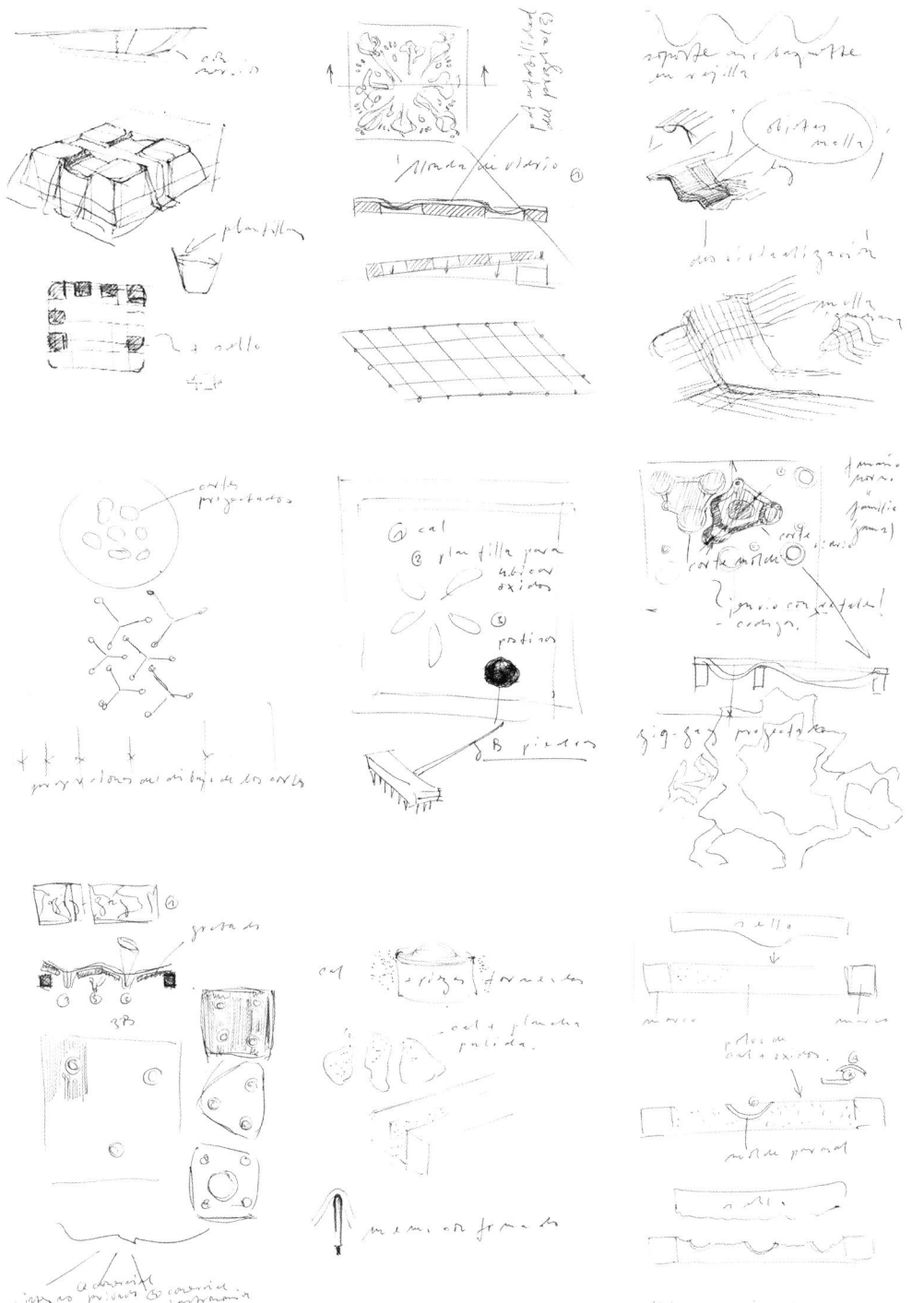

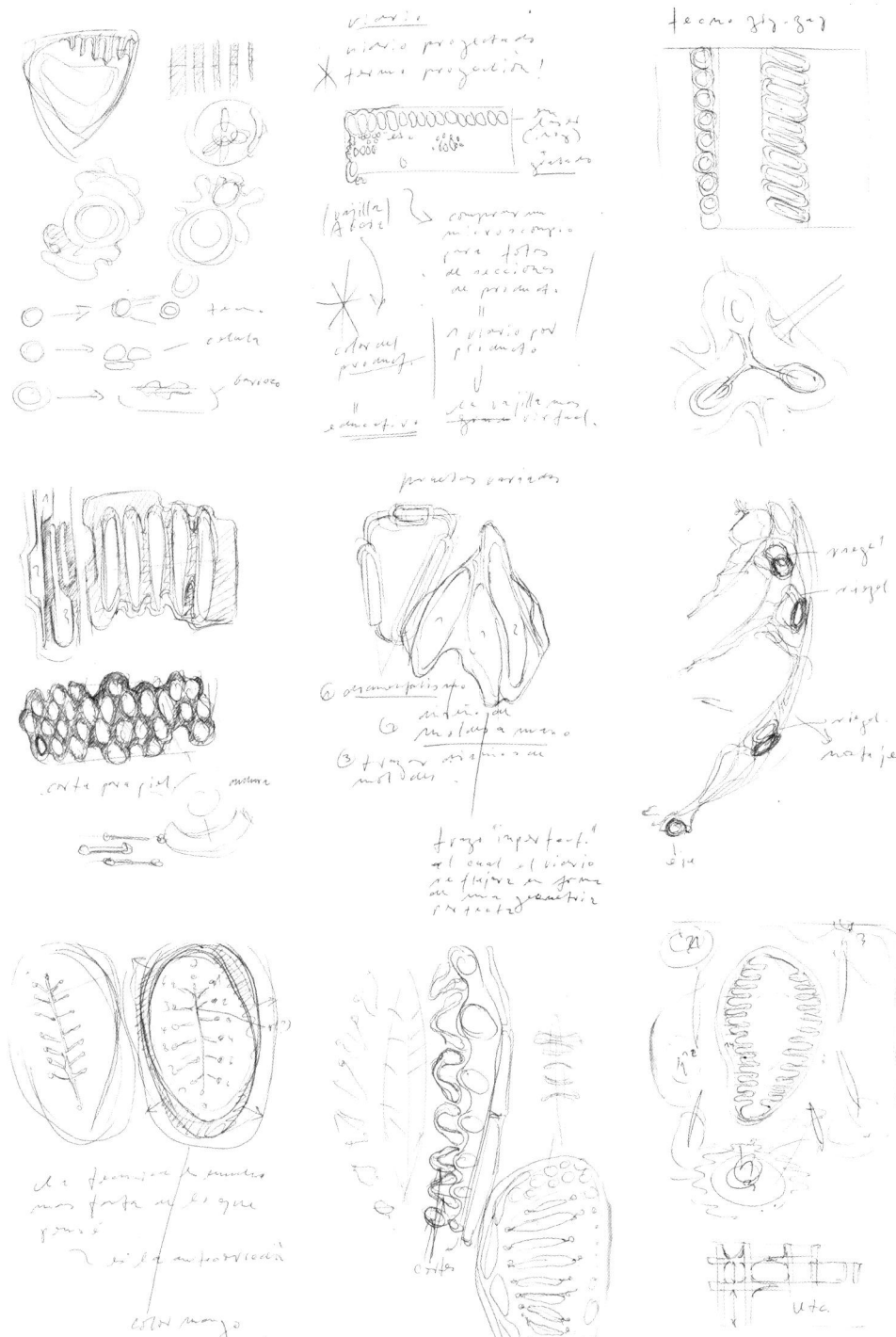

Thank you for your visit

In practically any bar in Spain it is common to find paper napkins printed with the words GRACIAS POR SU VISITA (thank you for your visit). But this isn't typical in fine-dining establishments. I thought it would be fun to reproduce this on paper, with the same dimensions as the folded napkin, but made by hand and embossed, for a touch of refinement and elegance.

The production process consisted of applying cellulose over a mesh and leaving it to dry. Victoria Rabal, director of the Molí Paper museum in Capellades, placed a vinyl stencil on the mesh with the words, with the result that less cellulose was deposited over it and the paper turned translucent.

This napkin was used to hold food.

GRACIAS POR SU VISITA

Thank you for your visit

GRACIA POR SU VISITA

Wasser zücher

Jamais serviette
etc - PAC.

Paper tableware

In order to make this paper tableware,
I had stainless steel mesh stamped so
that Victoria Rabal could use it to work the
paper, obtaining three-dimensional paper
products.

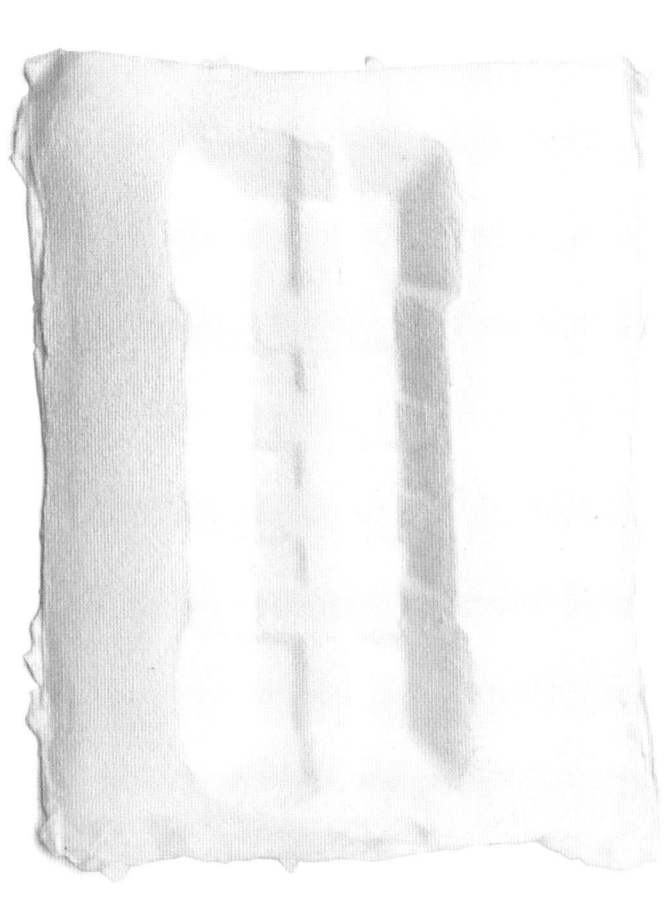

Paper tableware

Glass doily

Whenever the reservations system allowed, people would choose a date to dine at elBulli, and very often they would choose their birthday. This meant that almost every day somebody was celebrating their birthday.

At elBulli, we thought that it would be a good idea to add to this celebration, but given the patrons had just finished a tasting menu, it wouldn't be right to offer a cake, or even a piece of cake, which would be too big.

So it was decided that something very light but which appeared to be very large should be served. For example, one of Albert's ideas was to use stiff plastic, pour chocolate over it and, while it could still be moulded, roll it up into a spectacular creation.

As we needed something to serve it on, I screen-printed the typical paper doily used in cake shops onto a translucent glass platter with a small text (HAPPY BIRTHDAY ELBULLI), which produced the desired effect.

FACES series

▰ Industrial version

The FACES project arose when Neus Canal contacted us with the idea of a commercial line in collaboration with Cunill Orfebres. To give the line more impetus, other designers were invited, which meant that the brand would not be limited to reproducing elBulli's own designs. The other designers, who contributed with designs exclusively associated with cooking and serving, were Xavier Claramunt, Toni Arola, Martin Azúa and Júlia Mariscal. The graphic designer for the line was Pati Núñez, who had the idea of giving prominence to faces on the packaging, those of Ferran and the designers. This gave rise to the name FACES.

This project enabled me to once again work with silversmithing, which was fantastic for me as I had previously been a jeweller. Working with the silversmiths at Cunill gave me the opportunity to make all the spatulas by hand, in addition to the baroque platters, both for use as receptacles in themselves and as moulds for glass. I also made the meringue boxes there. While working on FACES, and outside of the project, I made other pieces, such as the adapter for the caramel spring, and the 'nitro-teppan'. As I've pointed out previously, FACES was the project that came the closest to bringing the designs for elBulli to the world of mass-produced industrial design.

Peg spoon

Kellogg's spoon

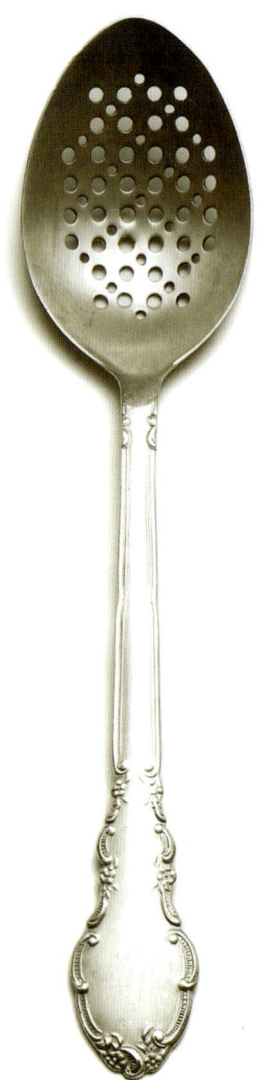

Baroque skewer

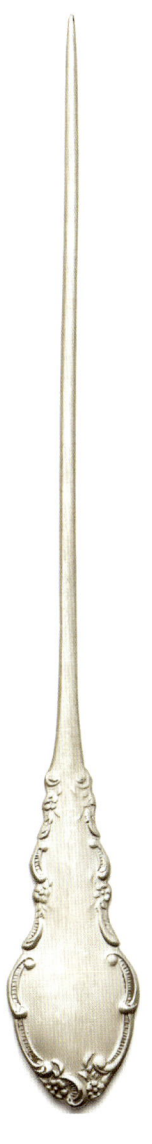

Ice-cream spoon
Coffee spoon
Medicine spoon

Tweezers

Sketches for FACES

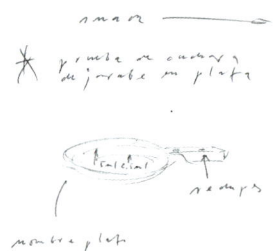

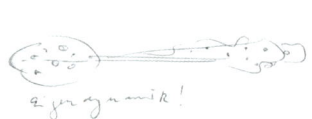

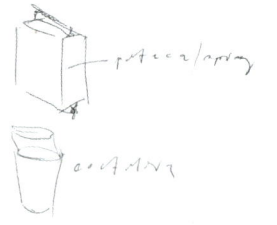

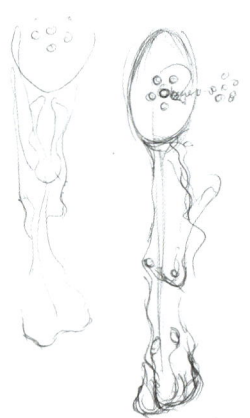

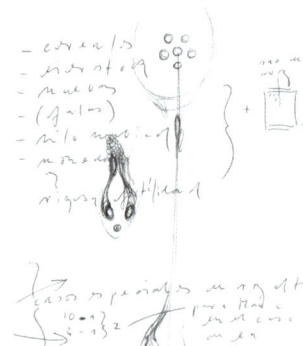

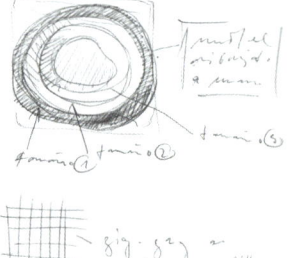

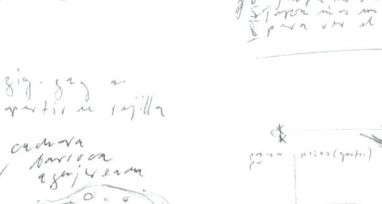

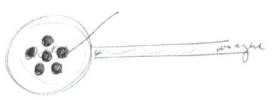

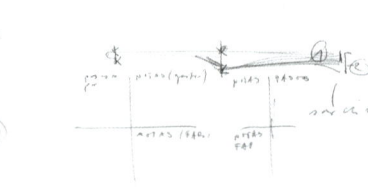

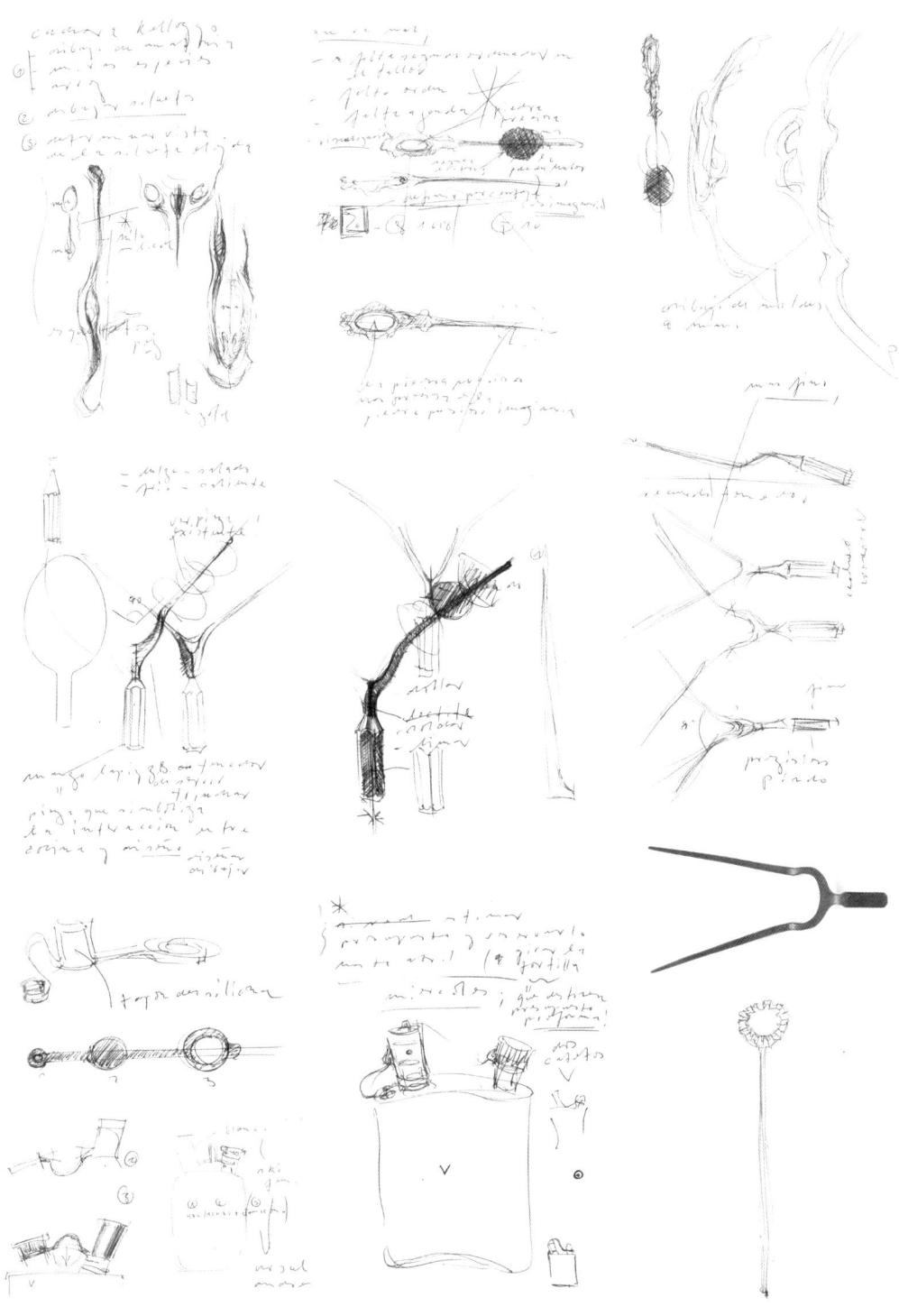

Skewers

A study on skewers and other utensils
for serving snacks, for mass production.

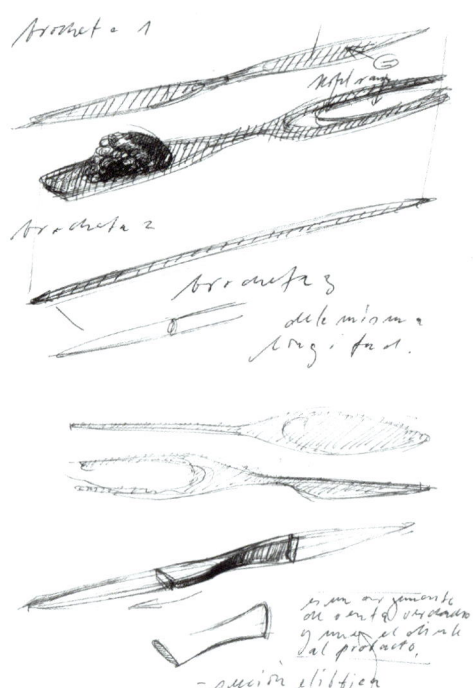

Dehydrated slice straws

These are straws made from dehydrated
slices of different products. For instance,
you could roll a slice of beetroot around
a stick and dry it out to give it the form
of a straw. The closest this came to seeing
the light of day was the vanilla pod used
as a straw.

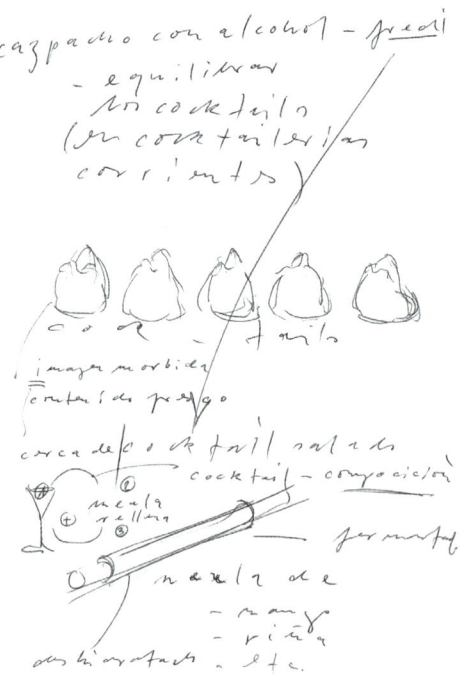

Suction cups for slices

The shape of this suction cup came about in response to the idea of it holding chips or the dehydrated slices of certain products.

Cock Tail

This is a play on the words *cocktail* and '*cock tail*' the tail of a cock or rooster. With this idea in mind, I bought a chicken, made a mould from it, and ordered items in thermoformed glass that were to be used as receptacles. In short, a *cock tail* for serving a cocktail.

Shot glass lid

The idea was to serve a liquid in a glass
covered with a lid that allowed the liquid
to pass through. The lid would hold a crisp,
which would be moistened, like cereals with
milk.

This concept had been realised in a
different form at elBulli in 2001 with the
paella Rice Krispies, which introduced
puffed rice into a broth, while in this case,
I only wanted the rice to be moistened
as it reached the mouth.

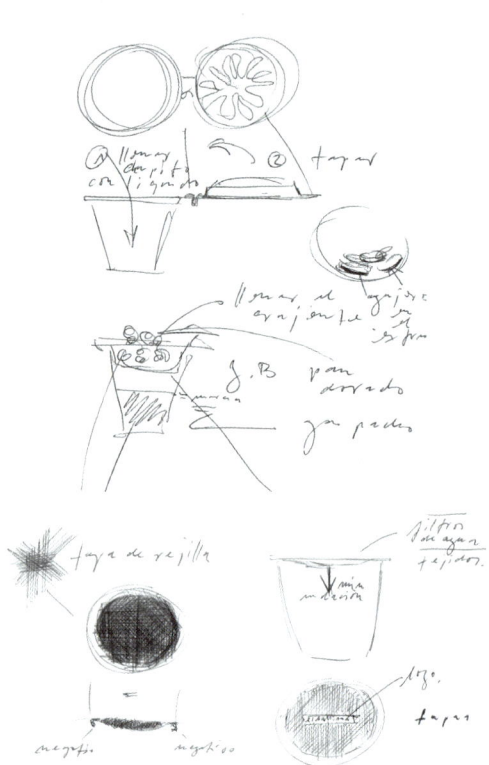

Passion-me coffee cocktail shaker

Sketch of the Lavazza cocktail shaker. Its
design was later commissioned by Lavazza
in Italy.

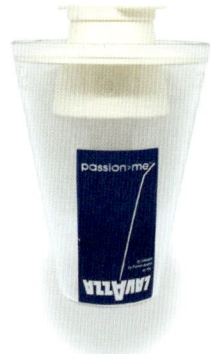

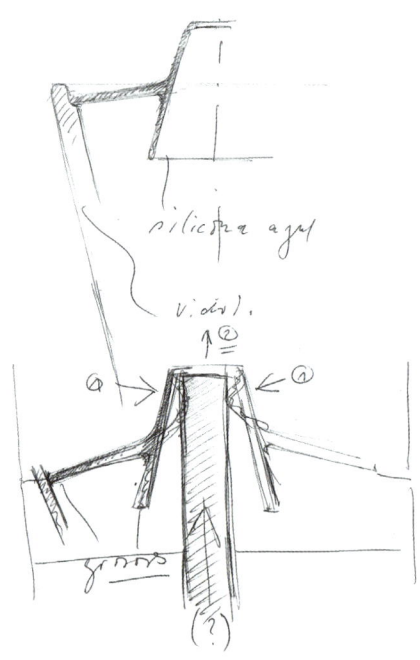

Industrial version designed by
Claudio Caramel.

Transmaterialised peg

Based on the transmaterialisation of plastic into silver, this design for a metal clothes peg could serve, for example, to hold a basil leaf or other products. If using a fresh basil leaf, it can become a spoon, and in this case the peg would be the handle.

When the commercial version of the fragrance spoon was made, we returned to the idea of the peg as an icon to show that the spoon could not only be used as a spoon, but also to hold objects.

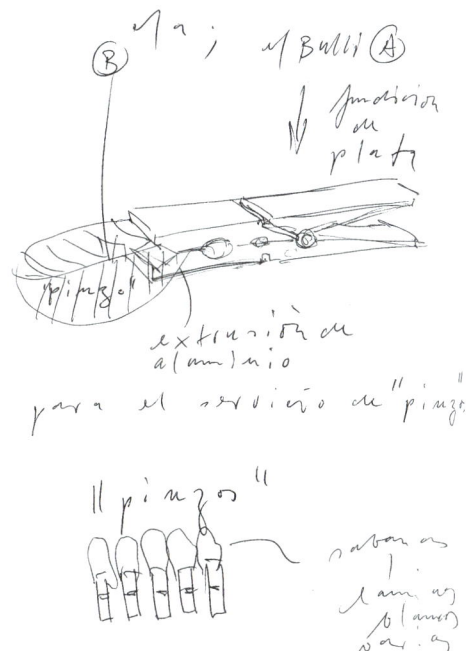

Calippo shot glass

This is based on the idea of making a soft food holder, so that diners could eat a preparation as if it were a Calippo.

Tea bag with flavour tag

This is a typical bag used to contain herbs for tea, however the paper tag also becomes a necessary part of the preparation by adding hints of flavour, making it necessary, naturally, to put the tag into the cup with the bag.

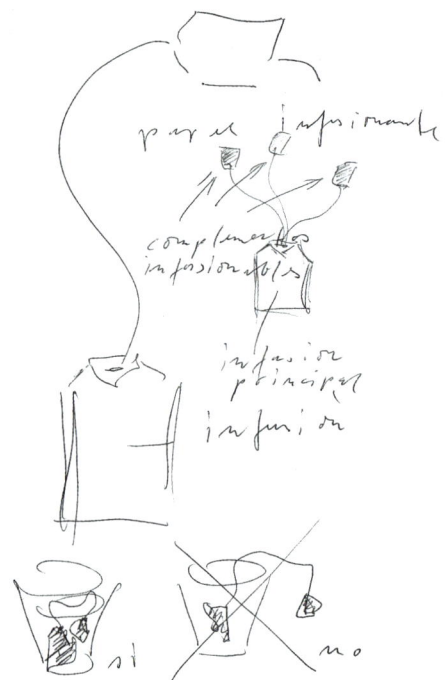

Black zigzag napkin

Starting with the typical folded paper napkin, we thought of hand-made paper, but coloured... black. I had heard that the director of the paper museum in Capellades, Victoria Rabal managed it with squid ink, but I was unable to see the result and so it wasn't used.

Tea bag
with Japanese leaves

As part of my investigation into tea bags
and the serving of tea, I came up with
the idea of making an organic tea bag,
after discovering these beautiful leaves in
a Japanese shop. These are leaves that
are processed, leaving only their veins,
their skeleton, making it highly porous. I
obtained a few leaves, filled them with the
ingredients of an infusion, and closed them
with a sewing machine.

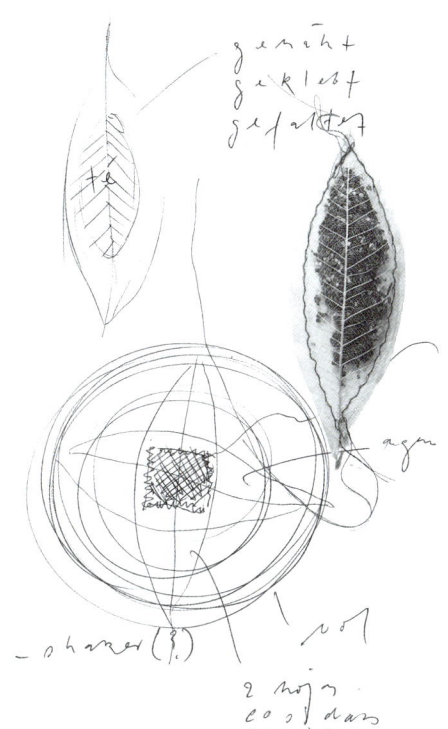

Cala Montjoi stone tweezers

I made these tweezers by joining three pieces
of slate with a rubber washer.

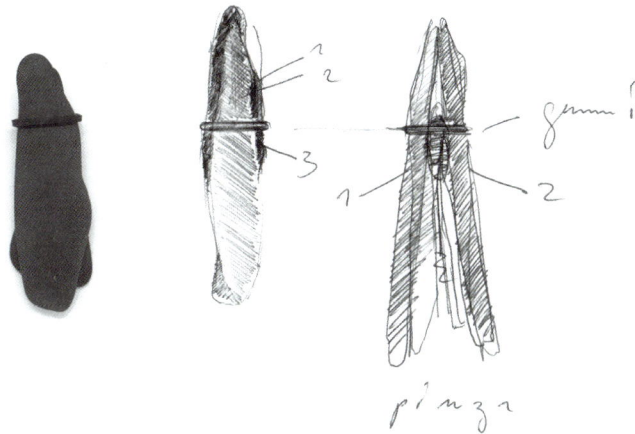

Martini glass with flavour rim

The rim of this Martini glass would be very flat, allowing the chef to place certain flavourings on it. The diner would drink the cocktail according to a pre-established order of sips for example, in order to make the most of the flavour combinations.

Steak knife with ceramic blade

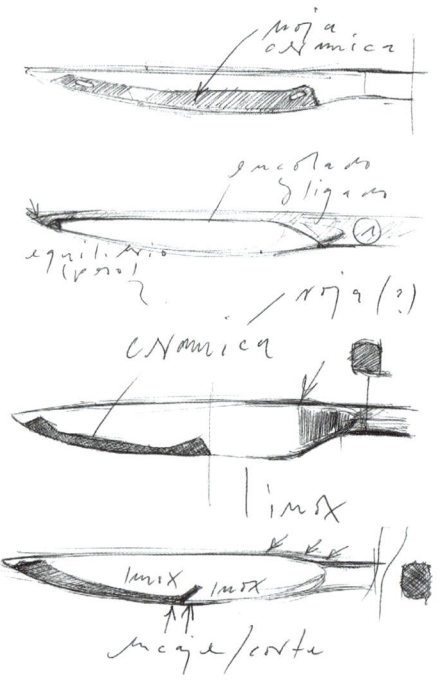

Ceramic knives had been in use in the kitchen of elBulli, and many others, for a long time because they cut very well. The idea was to make a version for use at the tables, perhaps not entirely of ceramic, but a hybrid. Actually, elBulli didn't serve cuts of meat that required such a knife, so this design belongs to the world of commercial versions arising from the collaboration with elBulli.

Geometric papillote packet

This design is a part of the gigantism concept, and consisted of serving diners a large papillote packet, which would be opened in front of them at the table. This packet was made using laminated material, a combination of aluminium and plastic.

It was another way of extracting the most of the aromas. When this packet in the shape of a cube, the top of which was at the same height as the nose, was opened, it released the aromas it contained all at once.

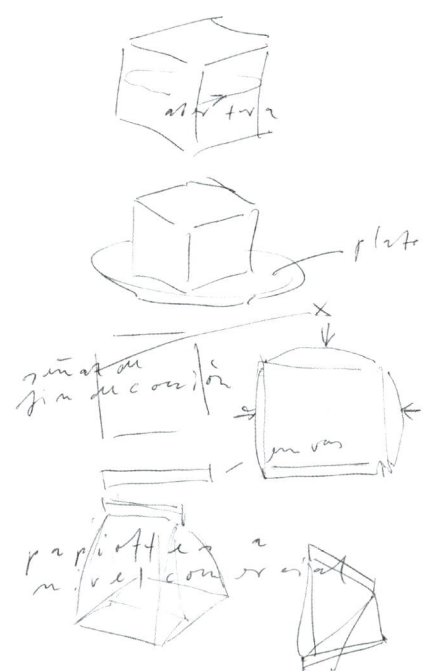

One-piece cocktail shaker

The advantage of this silicone cocktail shaker is that it is all in one piece. Because of the qualities of this material, one end can be flattened and the other folded, allowing the ingredients inside to be shaken without leaking out. The finished cocktail is then served from the cocktail shaker.

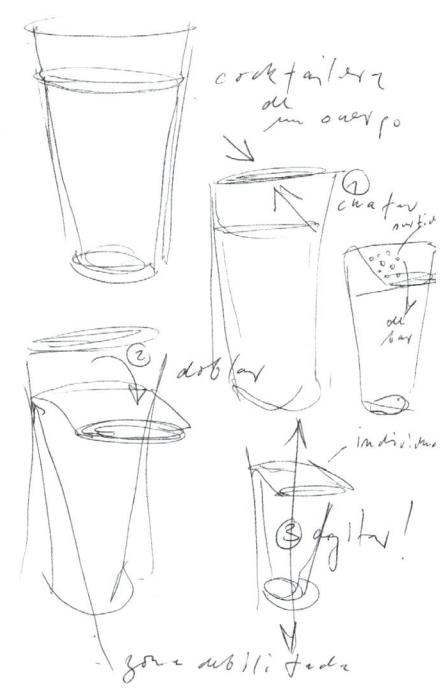

1   Nigiri spatula
2   Paper tableware
3   Silicone tableware

4   Basket bowl
5–6 Blown glass

7   Stackable cold-hot food holders
8   Zigzag tableware
9   Mini fondue pot

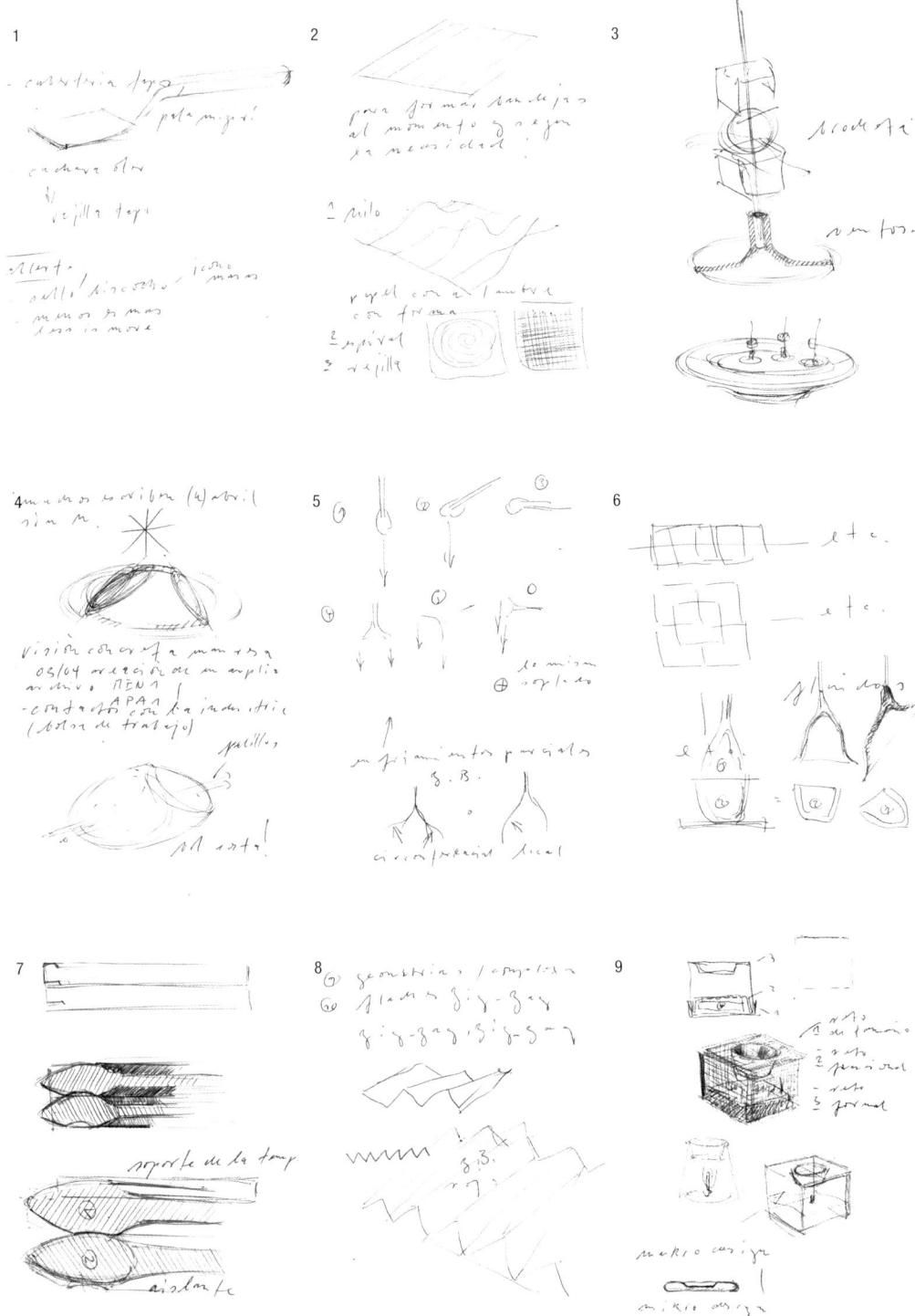

1-3   Aroma straw

4   Fragrance spatula
5   Fragrance tweezers
6   Fragrance bowl

7   Martini glass with flavour rim
8   Microspoon
9   Compass flower pot and skewer

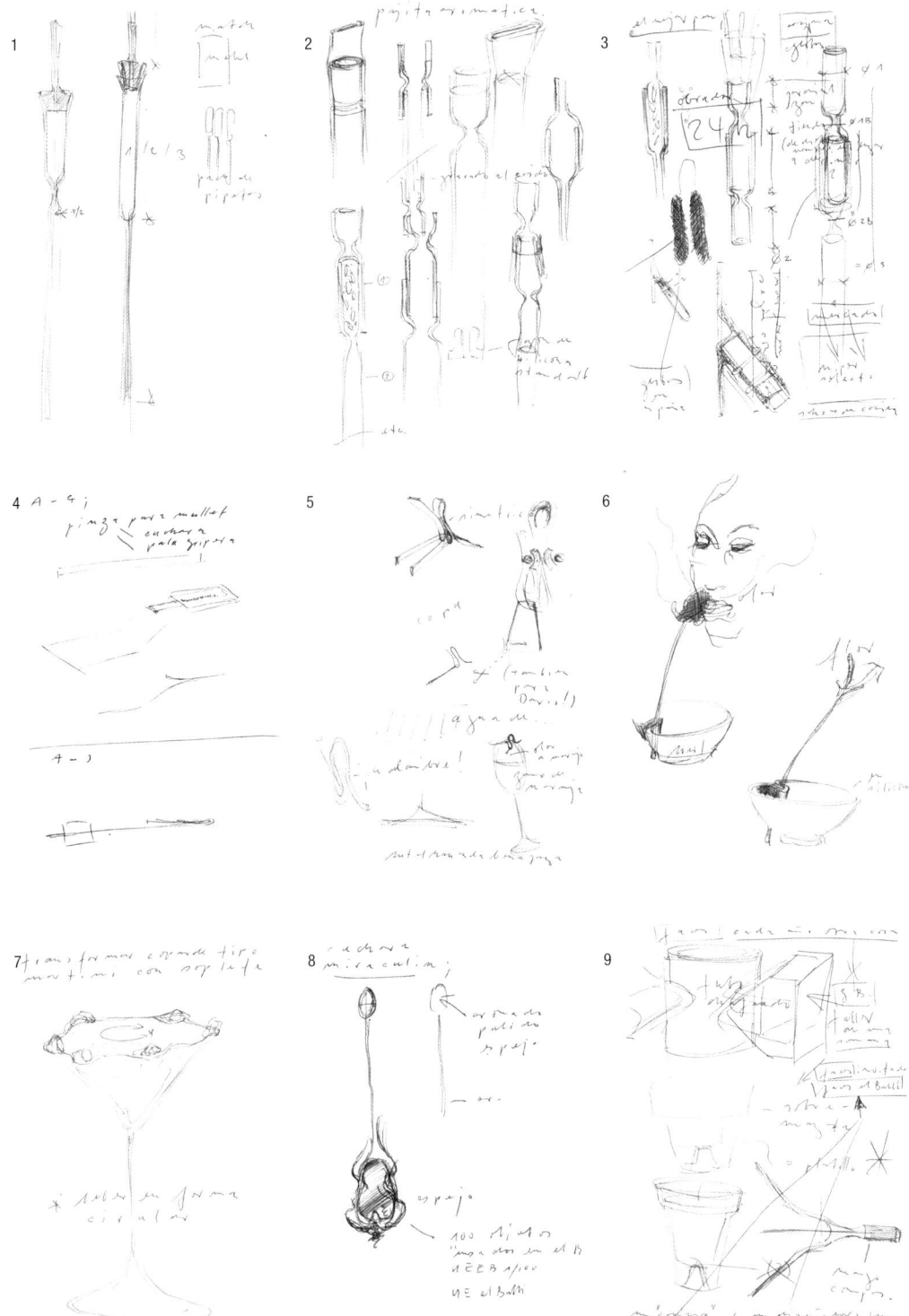

Found objects
for serving

During the first collaboration, we had already realised that we could have access to things that already existed, which was partially a response to the difficulty of creating limited editions. This realisation opened the doors to our turning to existing objects being used outside the field of gastronomy. Subsequently, by arranging them into subfamilies, according to the field in which they were found, what we were doing was opening up different sources of supply that would solve the answer to the question 'where else can we find objects of interest for gastronomy?'

Laboratory

Medicine

Packaging

Party supplies

Pipette

This item emerged as a serving utensil as the result of a mistake, and because of this I feel special affection for it. At the time, Darío Sirerol, a fragrance designer, was collaborating with elBulli and, in order to carry his liquid essences, he had a bag filled with pipettes, a laboratory implement with which I was unfamiliar. The point is that a certain chef saw this bag full of pipettes and must have thought that it was 'one of Luki's oddities', and so he left it on the shelf where I kept my experiments.

When I saw this object, I thought it was phenomenal for carrying liquids, but because it was pointed, if the tip was cut diagonally, it would be possible to skewer products. It became the first skewer in the world to come with its own sauce. Of all the items I found, adapted or created, it is perhaps the one that is most used by caterers today, because it offers the possibility of so many interesting combinations. At elBulli, for instance, it was used as a skewer for a prawn while containing the sauce made from its head, or it could hold a tiger nut accompanied by an horchata (tiger nut milk) 'sauce', among others.

The advantage of the pipette was that it was very cheap. Moreover, it was very significant in our quest because it opened up to us the world of laboratory implements. I soon became aware of something fundamental: we could always look for laboratory implements because this was a very hygienic environment; what was suitable for a laboratory would also be suitable for a kitchen.

Pipette

⚒. Idea for an industrial version

After using a shop-bought pipette, I thought it would be interesting to design a pipette with a particular shape. The project didn't succeed for the problem we commonly faced: we would need huge quantities which we couldn't source, which finally led us to continue to use the pipette we already had.

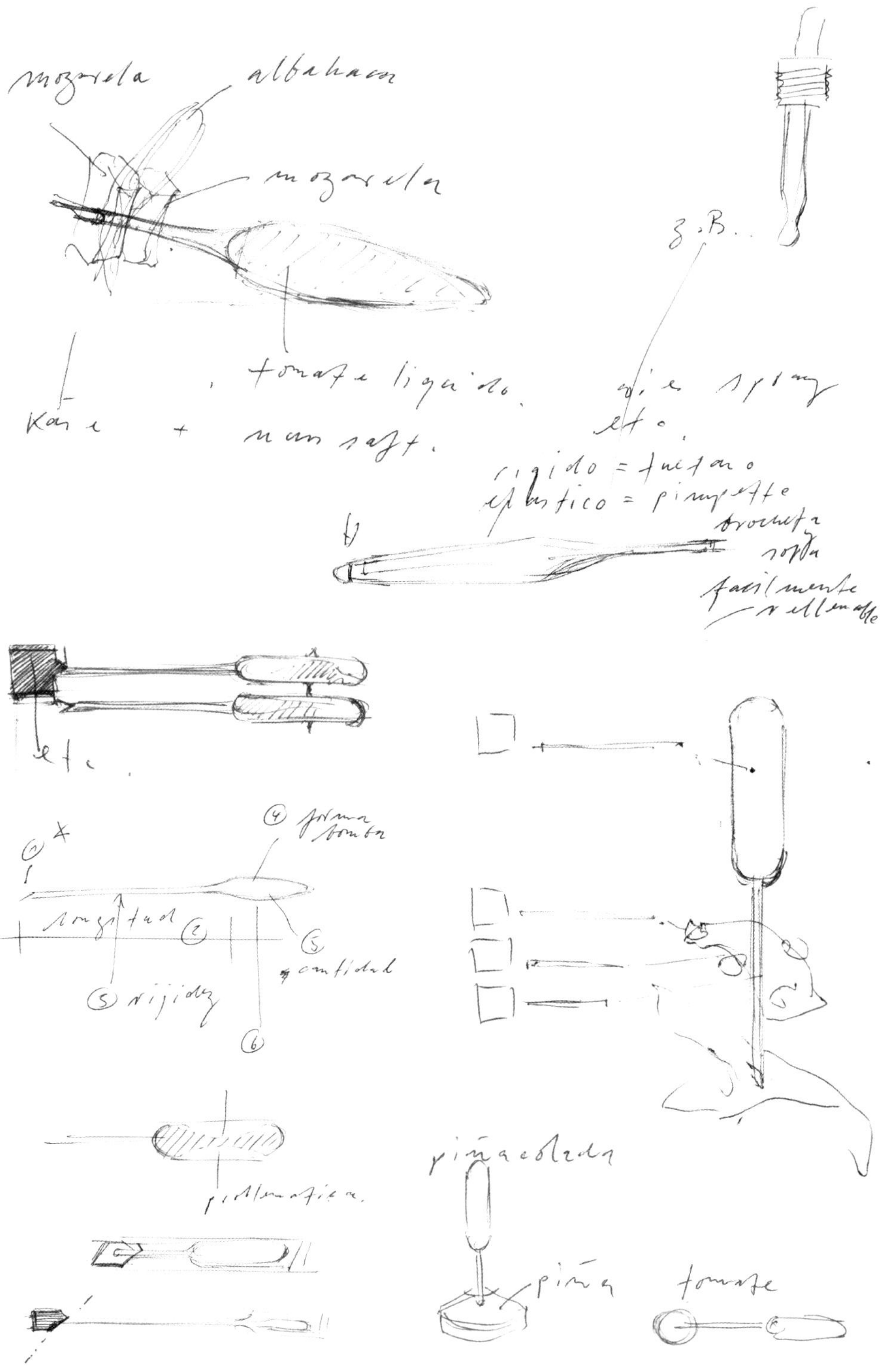

mozzarella   albahaca

mozzarella

tomate liquido.   oje spray
etc.

Käse   +   man saft.

rigido = tueiano
elastico = pinzette

brocheta
rolla
facilmente
rellenable

z.B...

etc.

④ forma
bonita

①
longitud   ②   ⑤ cantidad

③ rigidez   ⑥

problematica.

piñacolada

piña   tomate

Objects for serving preparations of varying consistency

. Idea for an industrial version

This chart of combinations between foods of different consistencies aided us in our quest for objects that could be suitable for serving them in each case.

By cutting a sniff diagonally, for instance, we would turn it into a skewer for holding a solid, which would allow diners to eat the solid part first and later to sip the jelly. Another idea was to introduce the pipette into the handle of a spoon to serve a creation to which diners could add the sauce as they were about to eat it.

Snack **X** comprising two food types of different consistencies	Amount of food equal to or greater than 1/2 **X**										
	Essence	Steam	Liquid	Cream	Purée	Gel	Foam	Powder	Crisp	Granule	Solid
Essence											
Steam											
Liquid						H3			H4		H2
Cream						H3					
Purée						H3					
Gel			H3	H3	H3		H3	H3	H3	H3	
Foam						H3					
Powder						H3					
Crisp			H4			H3					
Granule						H3					
Solid			H1								

(Left axis label: Amount of food equal to or greater than 1/2 **X**)

H1=soup-skewer, **H2**=sauce-skewer, **H3**=sniff, **H4**=lid (other cases to be defined).

3 pipetas.
3 pibometas.
3 pinzas.
3 cucharas.
3 capsulas.
3 cornetos.
3 tuetanos.
3 tenedores.

Π/E/F/G−J

pinchado

| con pinza.

||

cuchara con deposito

1/2 − c/2

elemento.   elemento
                   n/ollig adorc

pipeta

inyección
de plastico

Tweezers

Once I'd found that the world of the laboratory could be a source of supply, I realised that there was a shop just across the street from the elBulli workshop that sold medical and orthopaedic supplies, among other things. An excellent discovery. After that, I would often visit and I found a number of interesting things.

One of the items that over time was seen to have great use at elBulli was the tweezers used for changing dressings and for laboratory tasks. It was great for the dining room of a restaurant because it represented the Western way of eating very precisely, like chopsticks in the Orient.

In addition, these tweezers in particular have an incredible form. Thanks to their double curve, the tip never touches the table, which is an essential point in both food service as it obviously is in medicine for reasons of hygiene. When the tweezers are laid on the table, the curve substitutes the rest used for chopsticks. Together with the pipette, the tweezers are one of the items that is most seen today. You only have to flick through the pages of a culinary catalogue to see just how popular they have become. Tweezers, furthermore, are also used a lot in cooking.

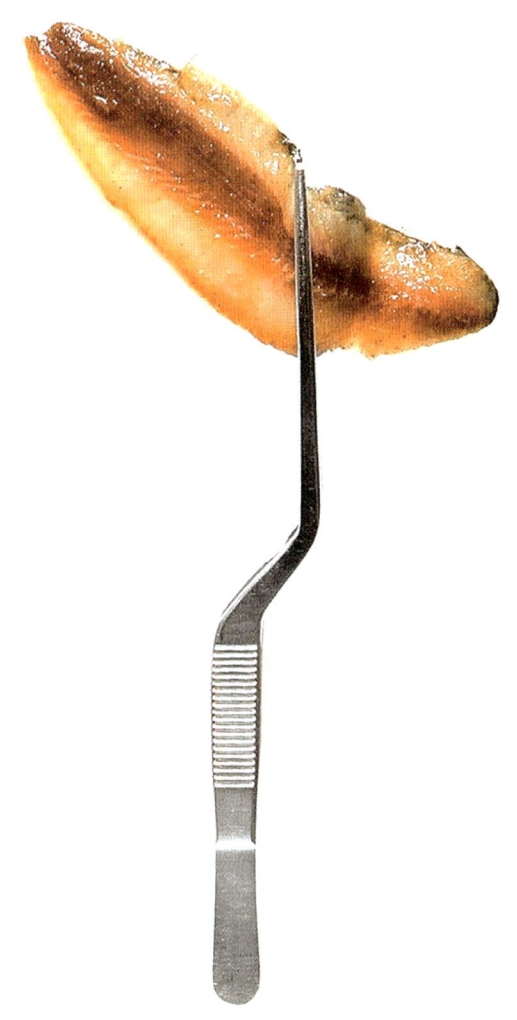

Project for own tweezer design

⬛.. Idea for an industrial version

This sketch is a study for the purpose of making our own tweezers. In theory, what I wanted to avoid was the serrated surface which, while providing greater grip, made cleaning difficult. The sketch of the trident tweezers on the following page is also a part of this project.

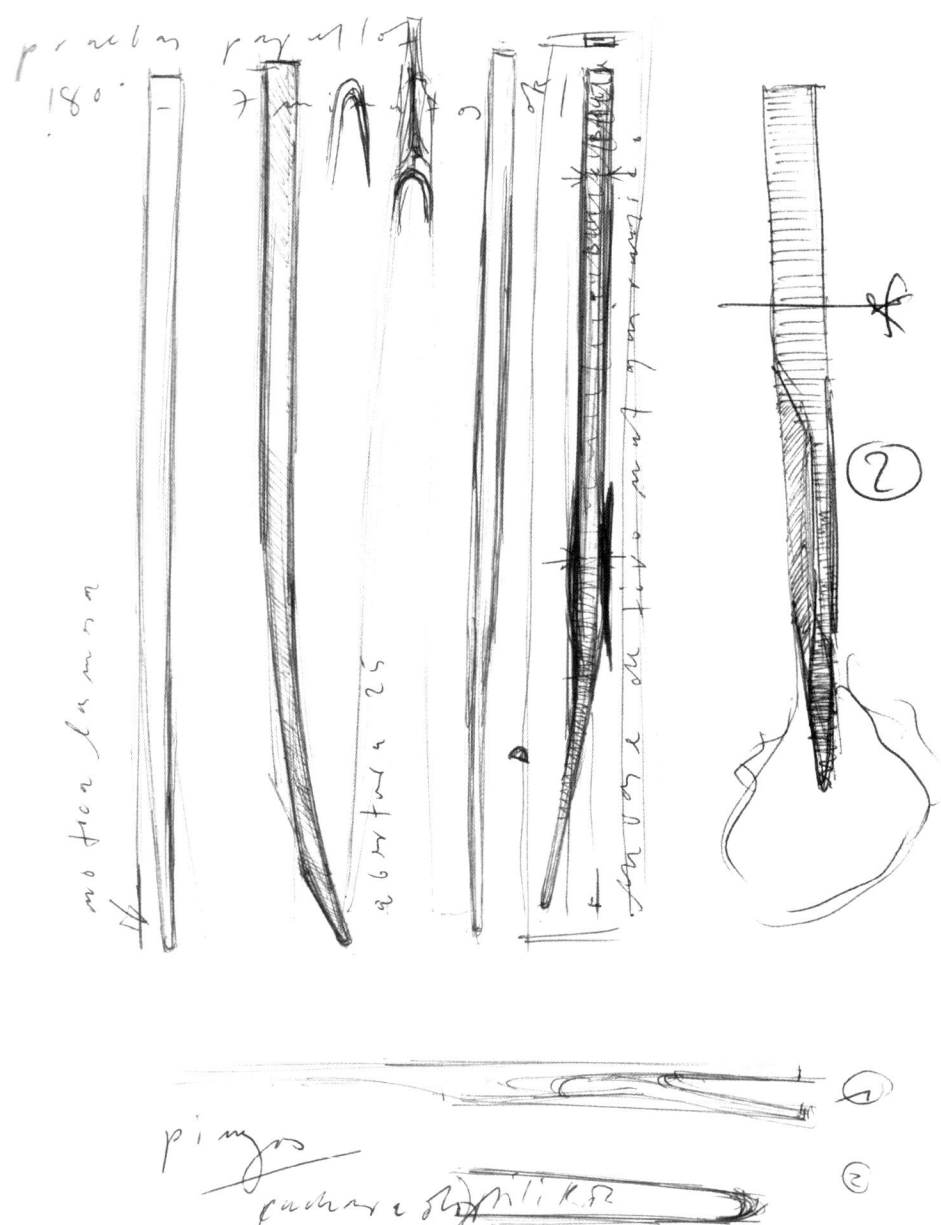

Trident tweezers

⬛. Idea for an industrial version

This design was an effort to do away with the serrated surface typically found on tweezers, which allows it to grip the object on which it is used. This solution would replace it through a different configuration of the tip of the tweezers, so that the two small teeth on one of the arms would interlock with the single tooth on the other arm, allowing the product to be held tightly. The advantage of this over the conventional tweezers was that cleaning would be easier.

pinzas tridente;

fácil de limpiar,

a la vez que ofrece
pma agarre!

¡centrado!

3 puntos | no toca a la mesa

0,3

% Tongue depressor

.. Idea for an industrial version

The percentage symbol that appears next to the name of this item is no error; it indicates that each tongue depressor included a percentage, a very small portion of a snack. There is a small hole in a tongue depressor where an entire snack wouldn't fit, so the idea was to serve several, so that their sum would form one hundred per cent of the snack. This object was actually never put to use, but it did pave the way for another family, the spatulas.

The amount and proportions of food served at the table have evolved greatly in the last fifty years. Before the arrival of nouvelle cuisine dishes were served on trays and large platters, etc. Nouvelle cuisine gave rise to plating in the kitchen. elBulli took this even further by creating spoons, an amazing utensil because the chef decides exactly how much of the preparation diners can put into their mouths. The tongue depressor, with its percentage of a snack, would come to be a subdivision of the spoon, with which the order of the components of a snack could be decided.

Stainless steel prototype

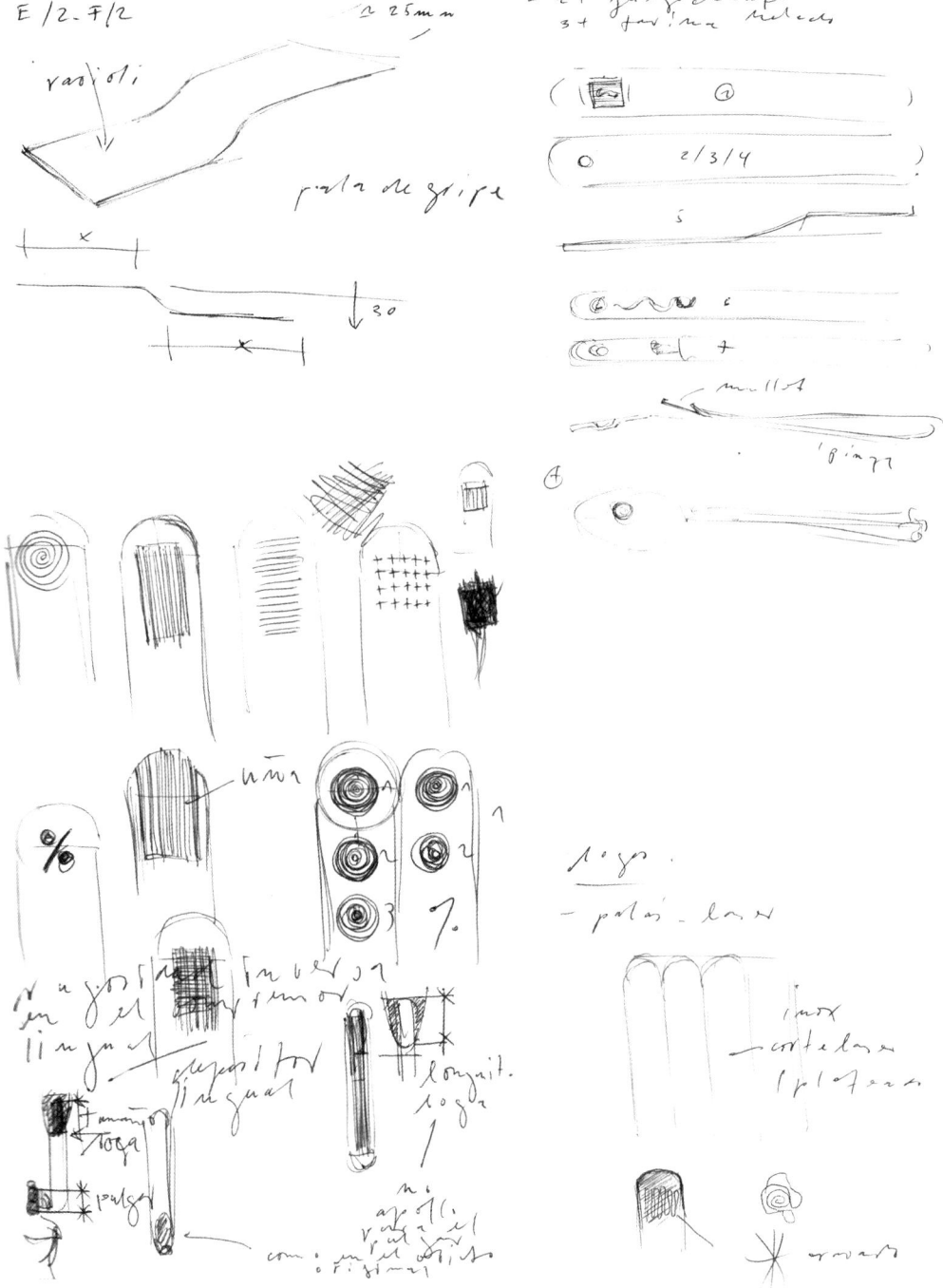

%

. Idea for an industrial version

The previously mentioned idea of the percentage represents the use of different receptacles or holders which, together, would add up to one hundred per cent. In this case, different sized portions would in a way constitute divisions of a dish.

For example, one could eat a dish in seven mouthfuls, starting from one part or another, or according to an established order. It also allows the proportions of ingredients to be varied. These spatulas have a space where diners can slide their fingers in order to pick them up.

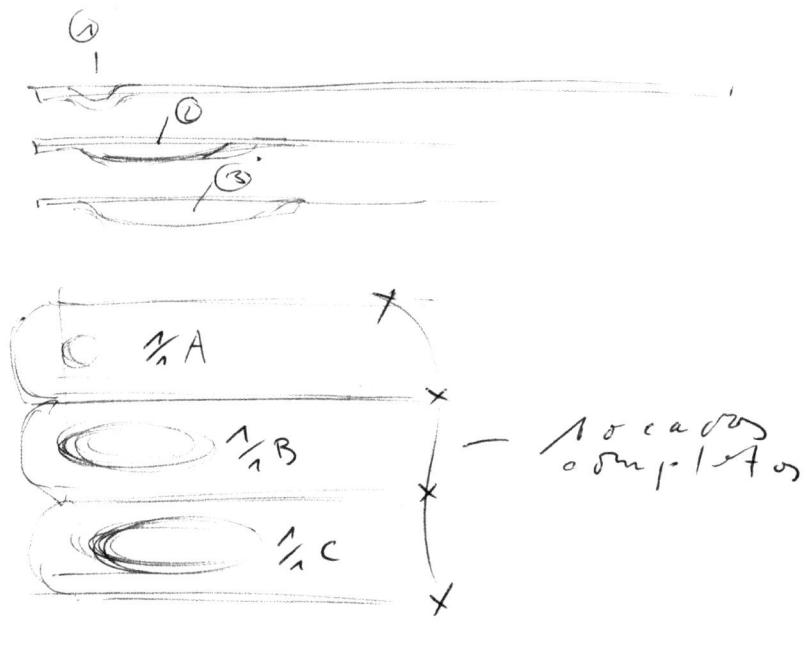

①

②

③

²⁄₁ A

¹⁄₁ B

¹⁄₁ C

} — bocados completos

z.B.
plato
y
cubiertos

cuchara (sin
ir (plato)_ sniff-
r i v e t a e t o)

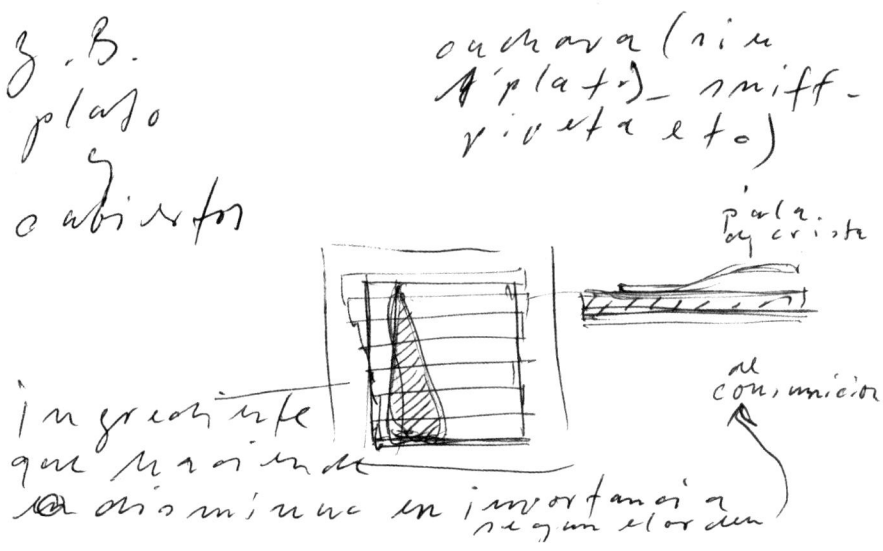

pala
o y crista

al
consumidor

ingrediente
que aumenta
(a) disminuye en importancia
según el orden

Self-closing clear plastic bags

This was an object I found and which we thought was ideal for holding dry snacks. It was actually a nod to another type of restaurant, to introduce a casual feel to haute cuisine. It also bore the elBulli label, a way of using graphic design to give 'brand' status to one of our own products.

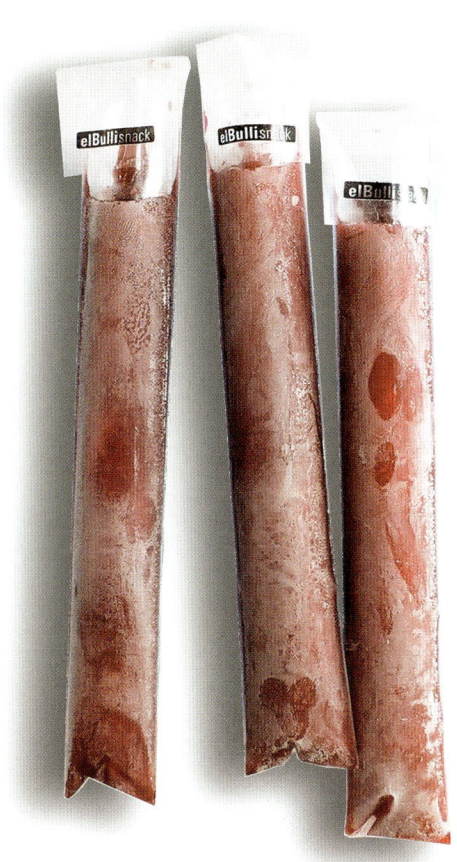

Diamond wrapper

This item marked a move away from laboratory implements and a foray into the world of packaging. In this case, it was the traditional wrapper used for diamonds and other gem stones. It occurred to us that we could use it to serve small, precious and delicate snacks to diners. For instance, it was used in 2003 as a wrapper containing soda and lime sugar pastilles.

Diamond wrapper

match

match / exportación
ou construons au
au rf.

Aluminium tube

This tube is normally used as packaging for pharmaceutical products. The advantage of this is that a specific pharmacy can order a small quantity of tubes to hold a certain product, meaning that it's sold with one end open, and that it contains a food-safe adhesive. This end is then closed and rolled up. Moreover, it would be quite economical to have it customised with the elBulli name.

It was mainly used in the restaurant to hold a rather runny peanut praline, with which diners could finish a dish. This was a process Ferran pursued in certain preparations, letting diners themselves 'cook' by adding the final flourish.

Caviar tin

elBulli turned to design when it was of interest to highlight a ground-breaking new creation. This case dates from 2003, the year spherification was discovered, and for one of its emblematic preparations, spherical caviar. We immediately thought that it needed something special to hold it.

At first, I attempted to design something new, that hadn't existed until then. In my notebooks there are a number of sketches for stone objects that didn't come to fruition. In the end, we thought it would be fun to use a real caviar tin, for which the Guzmán company assisted us in finding a supplier. What I did was to have the words IMITACIÓN ELBULLI (elBulli imitation) screen-printed onto it.

By the way, together with the silver-plated ice-cream spoon, the caviar tin was the item that most customers took home with them...

Spherical caviar holder

This was developed when spherification was developed. Given that it was a revolutionary technique, we wanted a special item in which to serve it. My first thought was to put a honed slate dish inside a caviar tin, bearing in mind the excellent thermal properties of this material. However, we immediately saw that it would be more amusing to use the tin directly, to reinforce the idea of caviar.

si la lata está rellenado solamente
con la piedra puede usarse
también como soporte caliente.

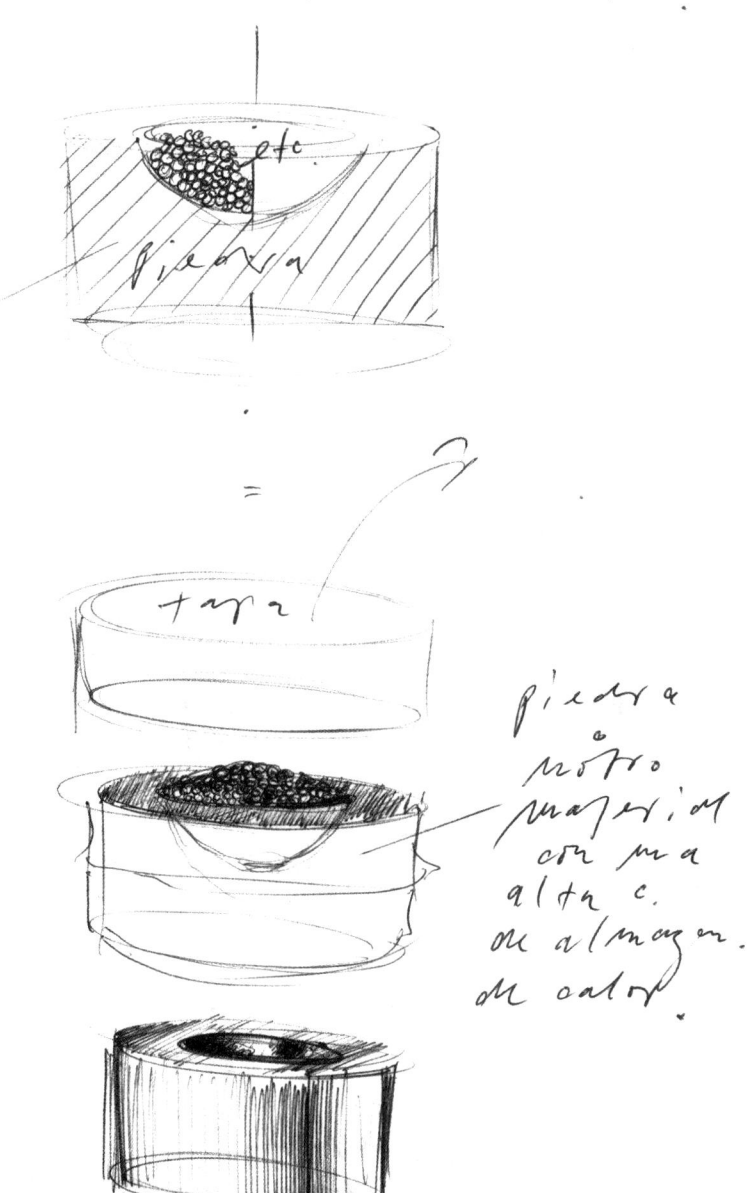

etc.

piedra

tapa

piedra
o
otro
material
con una
alta c.
de almacen.
de calor.

Baguette bag

There was an elBulli concept called gigan-tism, which consisted in taking large food items to the table in order to surprise diners. Actually, with such a long tasting menu as that offered at elBulli, if the chef was to provide a lot of preparations, they would have to be small, for obvious reasons. However, the gigantism family contradicted this rule, although only in appearance. Despite their large size, they were actually always very light preparations.

Among them was the *air-baguette*, a loaf of considerable size that was completely hollow; in other words, there was only crust. The idea was to put it inside a bag used to sell bread, each marked with the date, a reminder that the bread was freshly baked.

23 JUL. 2003

Graphic design for the baguette bag

The search for graphic design elements for the baguette bag. The solution chosen finally is shown on the previous page (the date).

fecha y hora

15 gr   .

PAN

¡ el pan de cada día !

¡ intervención gastronomía
¡ intervención de ordenie

Spray cocktail

While researching into the perception of taste and the textures of food and drink, we discovered that the experience of drinking something in the conventional manner is very different to that of spraying a specific amount of the same liquid into the mouth. So we experimented with filling atomisers with certain liquids, and we decided on cocktails, given their strength of flavour and the fact that they shared their content of alcohol with a perfume. It turned out to be a suitable resource, because empty atomisers can be purchased in the world of packaging, and there are no problems in terms of hygiene, because they can be cleaned and refilled.

Atomiser case

One way of giving identity to the atomisers
would be to custom screen-print a case,
or even the actual atomiser, as was done
on certain occasions.

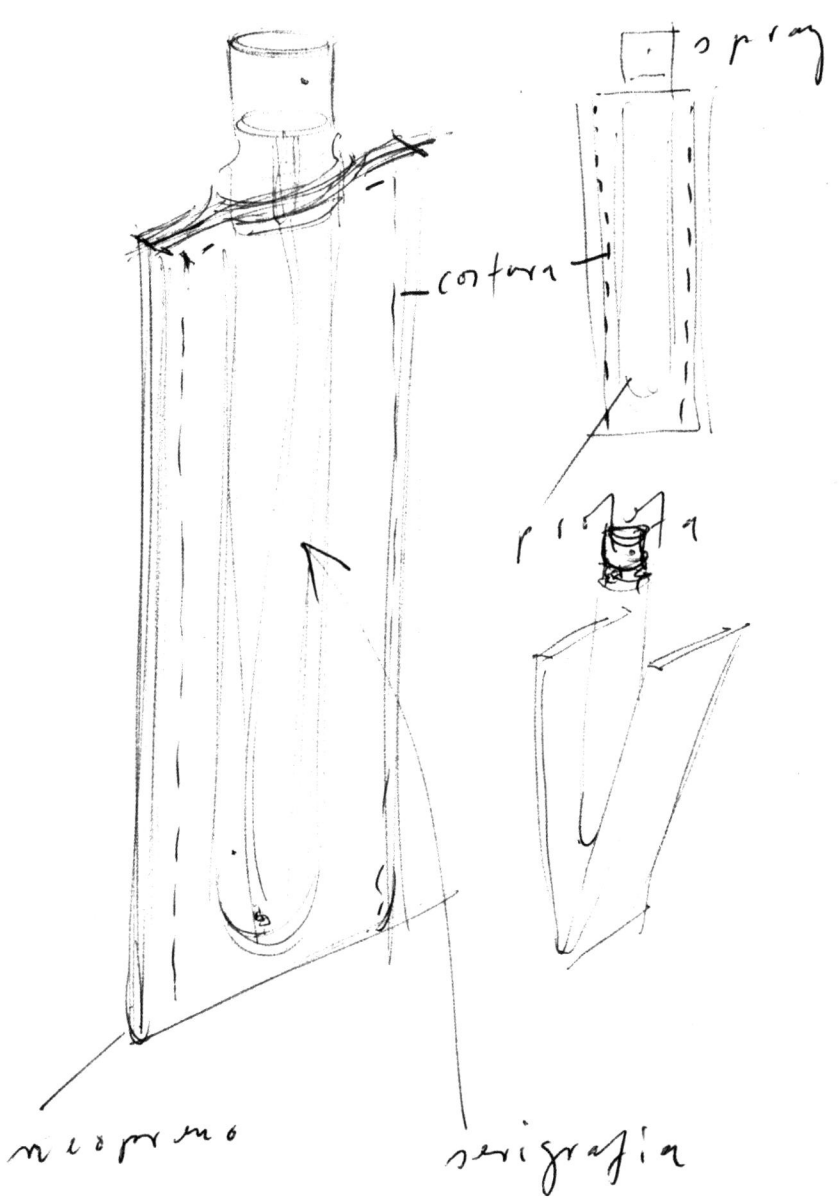

spray

cotura

serigrafia

neoprene

serigrafia

COMME des GARÇONS atomiser

Limited series of one hundred atomisers
made for a Comme des Garçons exhibition.

Hip flask spray

📇.. Idea for an industrial version

During the development of the FACES range, we played with the idea of designing a commercial version of the 'spray cocktail' idea. The resulting object would be a hip flask with two openings. One for drinking and the other to spray the liquid into the mouth. The project was finally ruled out. Although we thought it was suitable in the restaurant setting to serve a cocktail in spray form, we felt that it wasn't appropriate to propose a gift item for holding alcohol.

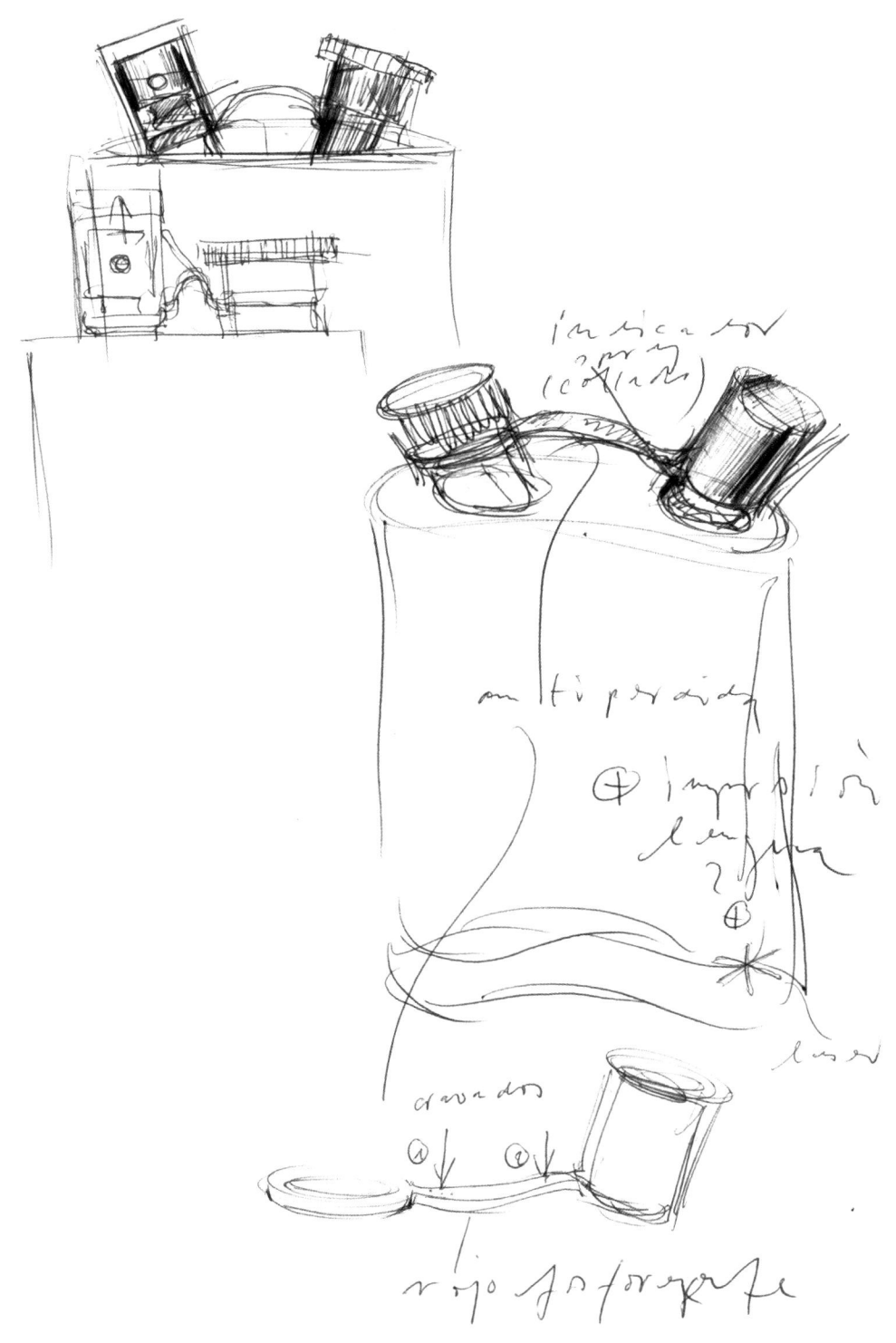

Tin loaf packaging with graphic design

Like the *air-baguette*, this design also came under the gigantism concept. It consists of a polystyrene container normally used to hold one litre of ice cream. This quantity was apparently exaggerated for a single preparation, but it actually contained frozen air, the ultimate in lightness. In 2003 it was made with chocolate air – which we called a 'tin loaf' – and a Parmesan air with home-made muesli in 2004.

The *mise en place* for this was very simple, because all the containers were filled for the meal service and put into the freezer. This 'found' object was complemented with a 'specifically designed' object, a sleeve for the label, with a graphic design by Marta Méndez Blaya.

'Home-made olive' jar

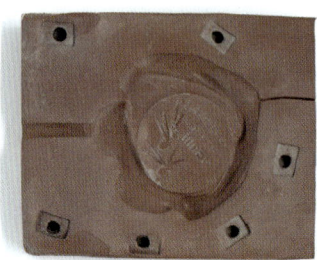

For the spherical olives of 2005, it occurred to us to use large glass jars with latch lids. I had a wax seal made which we transformed into bronze by means of a system similar to lost wax casting, which was used to decorate the lid.

'Home-made olive' jar

LACRE

ACEITUNAS
CASERAS
el Bulli

Jewellery box for spring

A box from the world of jewellery, adapted to hold the olive oil caramel 'spring' which was presented as if it were a ring.

Fragrance balloon

In 2004 some of the snacks and dishes were paired with aromas created by the fragrance designer Darío Sirerol. The method initially consisted of spraying the desired aroma (of a forest, the sea, etc.) in the space in front of diners, which would greatly enhance the experience. But there was a problem: perhaps something else was being eaten at the next table. This meant we had to think up a system of controlling the direction of the aroma, so that there was no distortion created for other dishes, and more importantly, so as not to ruin the surprise of this aromatic enhancement.

Consequently, I found this balloon, which has a very thin part at the tip, which allows different balloons to be joined together. A normal balloon explodes when cut or pricked, but because this one has a thin cylindrical tip, it could be cut with scissors or an elegant cigar cutter without exploding.

What we did was to fill the balloon with air and orange flower aroma, to accompany an orange nitro-sorbet. When the tip was cut, all the aroma would be released towards the diner, achieving the desired aromatic enhancement without disturbing diners on nearby tables.

Fragrance balloon

Bubble inhaler

The idea behind this inhaler was to create the equivalent of the typical soap bubble, but instead of making them by blowing, they would be made by inhaling. In other words, inwards instead of outwards. The idea was actually to make a single bubble that would fit the palate to create the world's lightest membrane.

When you blow, you make a small opening with your mouth to concentrate and direct the air released with force. In this case, inhaling a bubble would require the opposite action, opening the mouth wide and inhaling gently. In the end, I was unable to find a technical solution, among other things, because I couldn't find an edible soap.

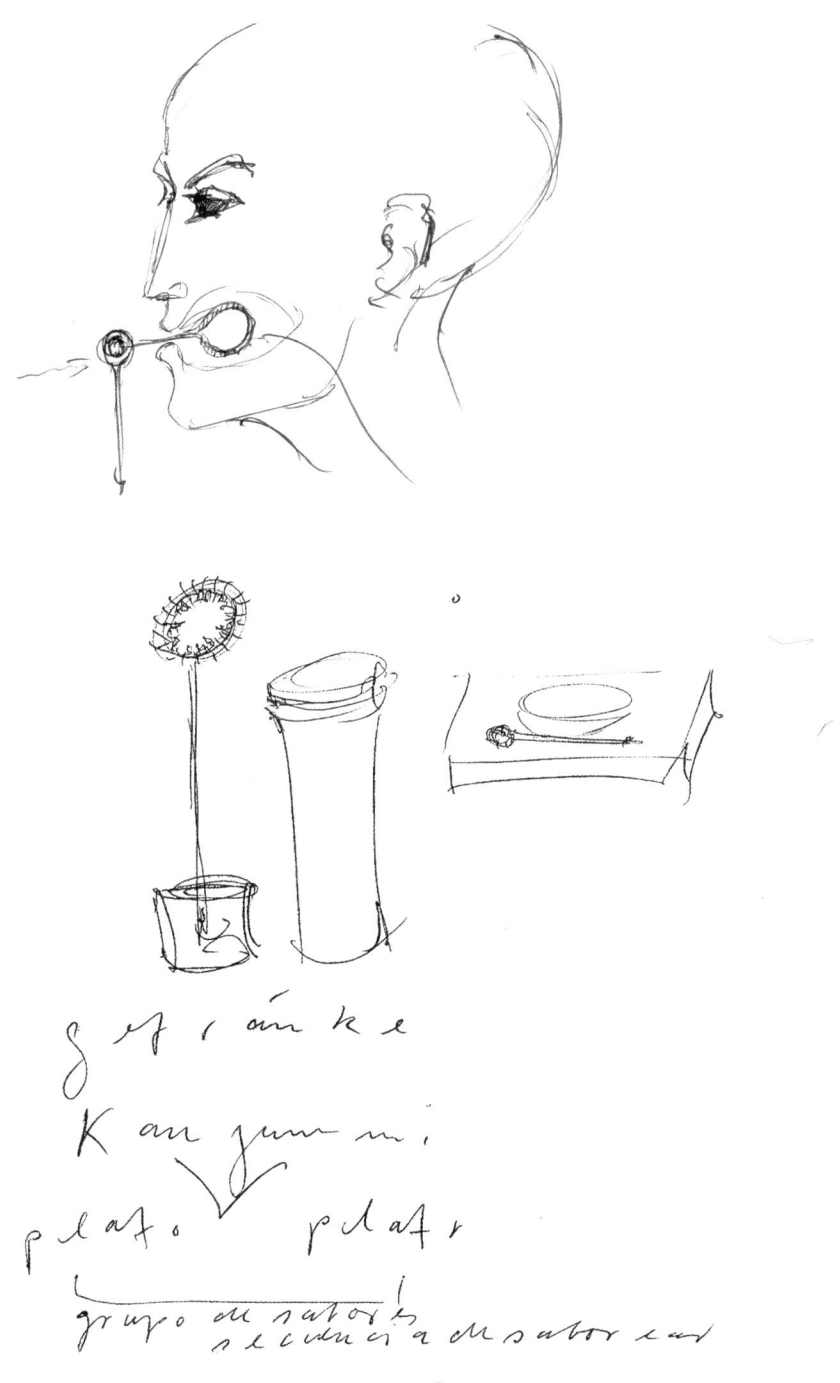

getränke

Kaugummi

plato → platr

grupo de sabores
secuencia de saborear

Serving soup using tea-making utensils

This series of designs related to a tea set comes under the heading of items that never came to fruition... or, to use the term used at elBulli, that were sent 'back to the drawing board'.

The idea consisted of using a metal tea infuser ball – or three in one bowl, for example – or tea bags and other utensils, but replacing the leaves for a concentrated stock, with which to create an instant infused soup.

Mate straw

A mate straw consisting of a tube with a filter on the end immersed in the beverage. This filter prevents stems, leaves and other solids from entering the tube when the liquid is sipped.

The idea was to apply this concept to other preparations made up of a liquid infused with solid particles.

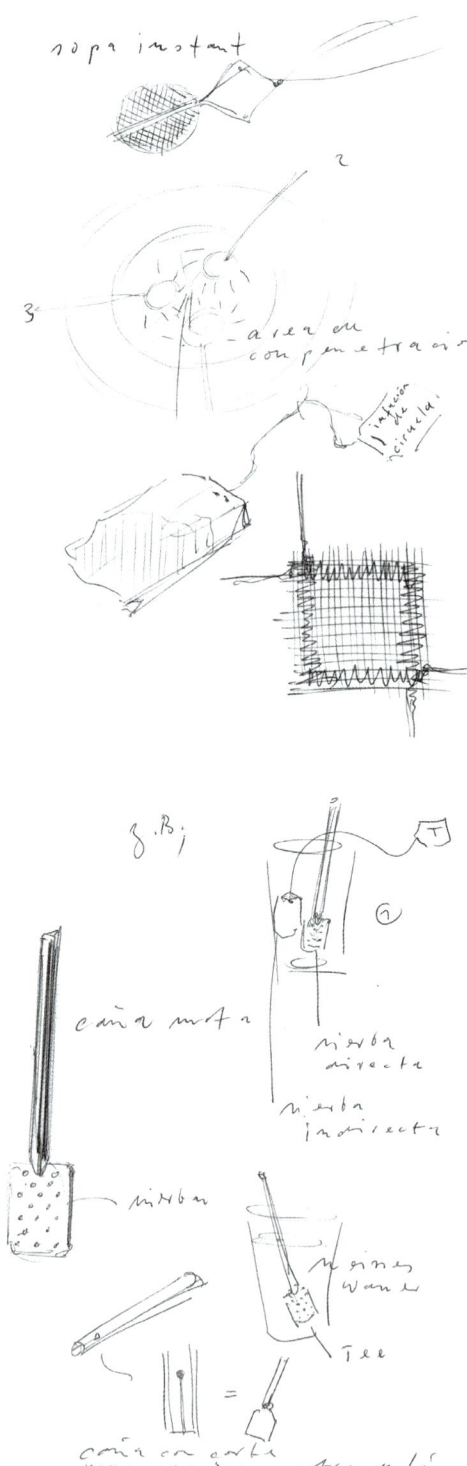

Wine glass for aromatic soups

Within the series of designs thought up to enhance the olfactory component of dishes, I thought at one time of serving highly aromatic soups in glasses, to give them an importance similar to that of wine.

Aroma glass

While insisting on the idea of enhancing aroma, I thought of a typical takeaway coffee cup, making use of the hole that is used to drink the coffee, but to be able to perceive the aroma first, before eating the preparation inside.

The German expression *Vorfreude* refers to the happiness that one feels when looking forward to a lovely event that is soon to happen. We feel something similar when we step into our grandmother's house and perceive the familiar smell of a stew that has been cooking away for some time.

This aroma glass aims to reproduce the same sensation, using smell as the way of giving diners an idea of what to expect.

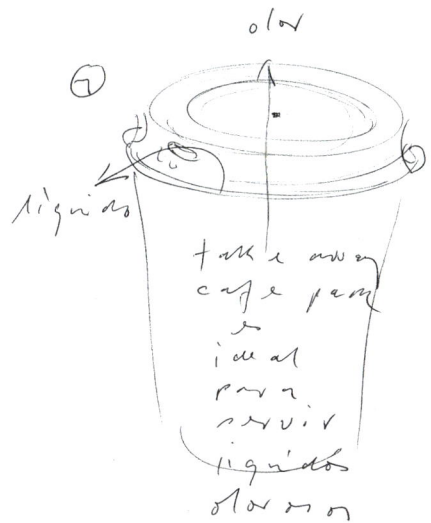

Galileo Galilei cocktail

In the late nineteen nineties, Ferran had already toyed with the differences in densities in a single preparation. In this case, by combining this concept with spherification, I came up with the idea of suspending different spheres in one test tube, with each sphere containing a different liquid whose density would cause it to sit higher up or lower down. It was a small test tube, so the contents could be eaten in a single mouthful. This test tube was inspired by the thermoscope, an invention by Galileo Galilei, in which balls of liquid with different densities floated at different heights.

Straw plug

The basic idea of this was to insert a straw into the peel of a citrus fruit, so that it remained inside the straw as a plug. In a similar way to the concept of the sniff, the contents of the straw would be sipped, allowing the 'plug' to be the first thing entering the mouth. Logically, the flavour of the liquid would have to be combined with the citrus peel.

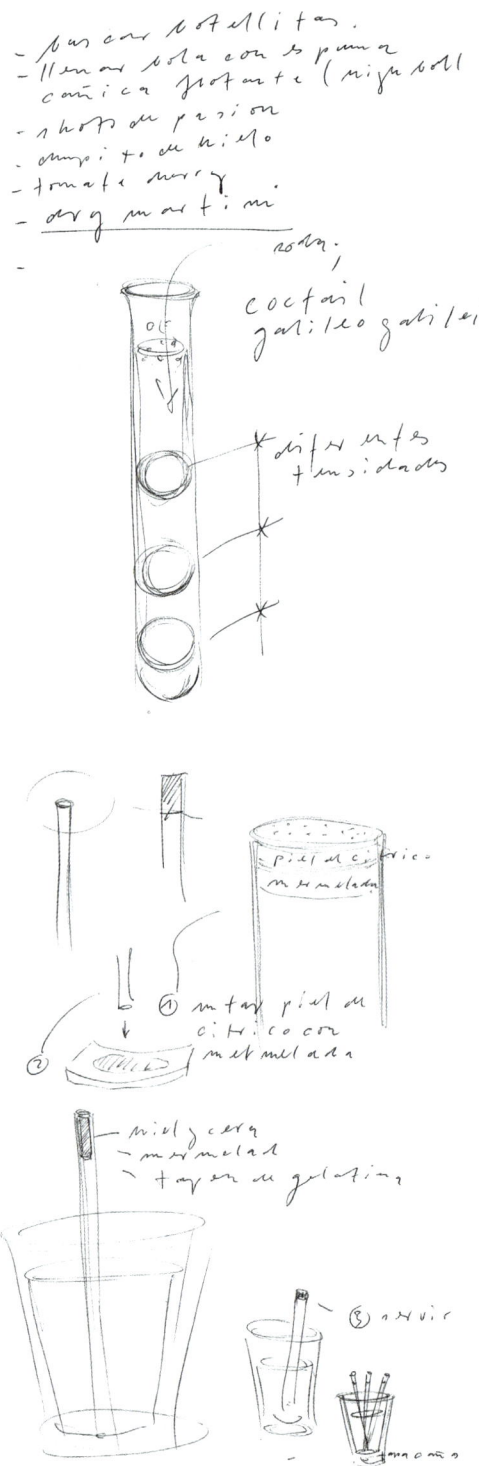

Test tube 'trivásico'

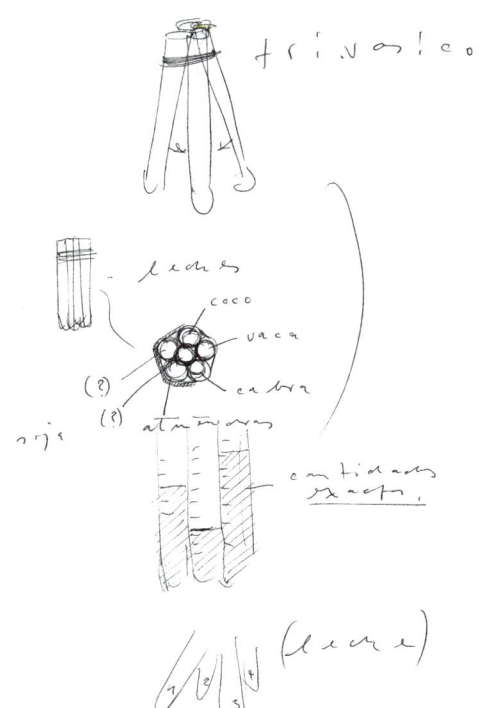

Here, there is an obvious play on words. The Spanish *trifásico* is a cortado, an expresso coffee to which a similar amount of milk is added, with the further addition of a brandy or liqueur, such as cognac, rum, whisky or anisette. The 'trivásico' [a play on the Spanish word *vaso*, glass] consisted of three glasses, or rather, three test tubes, each containing a specific liquid. When drunk all at once, the three liquids with different flavours, temperatures or textures would be savoured.

Pressed flowers and leaves set

The origin of this idea is a memory of childhood and the practice of pressing flowers in books to dry them and sometimes to leave their scent in the book. It all began because I pressed a slice of pineapple together with a flower inside a sketchbook. This idea also didn't come to fruition, although the flower paper of 2007 could be seen as a validation of the concept.

Basil leaf spoon

The term 'organic tableware' could be
defined as any object from nature (a leaf,
stone, nut shell, etc.) that can be used as a
receptacle. In this case, we wanted to use a
basil leaf, which when freshly picked is taut
and resistant, as a spoon to serve and be
eaten with a preparation.

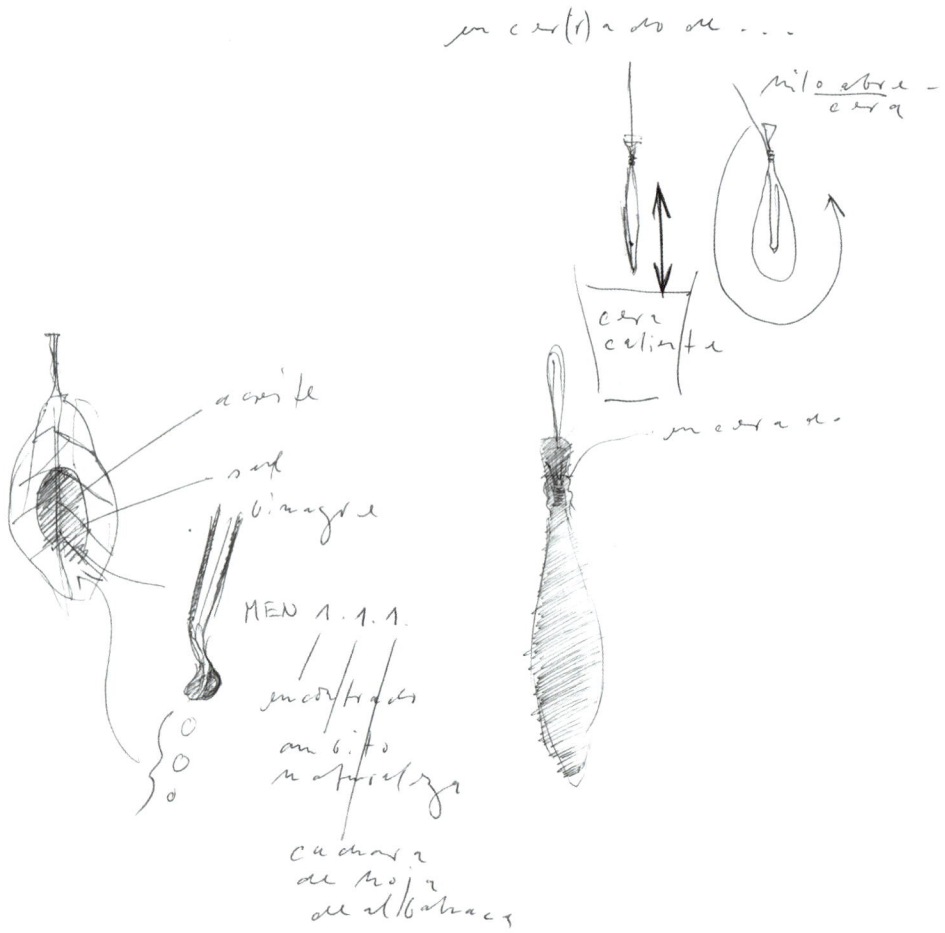

'Wax-coating' set

The famous Babybel cheese is protected by a coating of red wax. With this in mind, I wanted to explore the possibility of 'wax-coating' a product for serving in the restaurant.

One option for this idea was, when applying the hot wax, to cook the product by the actual heat of the wax, and/or to have the wax help to preserve or mature the product.

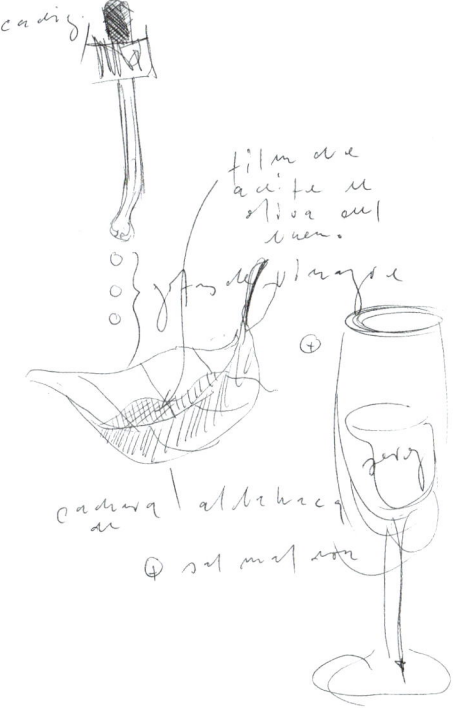

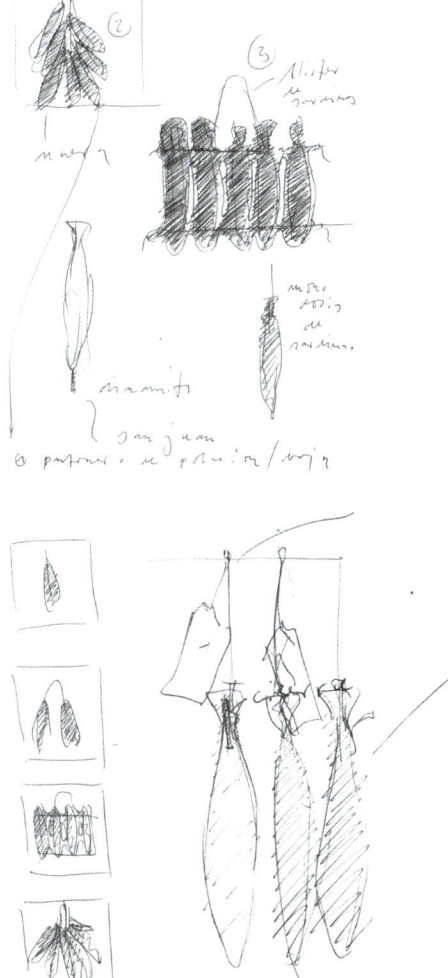

Found objects
for cooking

Once we realised we could resort to existing things for serving food, we also saw that we could do the same in order to cook it. One interesting fact is that if a restaurant like elBulli wanted to visit a trade show, it would in theory visit one held by the food industry, such as Alimentaria. But once we'd realised that we could use laboratory equipment, the one we would visit was Expoquímica, the international chemistry show, and so forth.

This chapter of the book has been arranged in the different fields from which the different objects came.

Laboratory implements

Pharmacy

Laboratory equipment

Ironmongery

Fairground equipment

Pipette

The pipette we began using as an object for serving, to be able to eat a solid product with its sauce incorporated, turned out to be a fantastic implement for cooking, particularly for applying sauces with the greatest precision. For instance, it was used to add sauce to the Parmesan *spaghetto*, a preparation that features several dots of sauce in different places over the plate.

Ravioli spoon

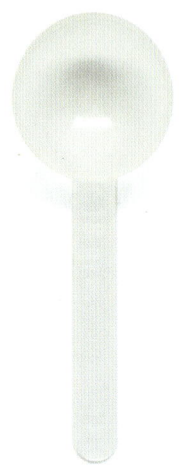

One of the first preparations made with the spherification technique were the tiny spheres comprising the melon caviar. However, larger spheres were also devised, such as the pea ravioli and the marble. In fact, the size of the sphere determined the name given to each spherification.

The ravioli could be made using any spoon but it was much more attractive if made with a hemispherical medicine spoon.

Ravioli sieve

This is an implement for taking spherical ravioli out of the calcium chloride solution. Its role was the same as that of a slotted spoon that was used more frequently.

This sketch was actually a response to the desire to achieve a very fine skin on the ravioli. In other words, after soaking very briefly for a moment in the solution, the ravioli required a utensil without the sharp edges of a slotted spoon.

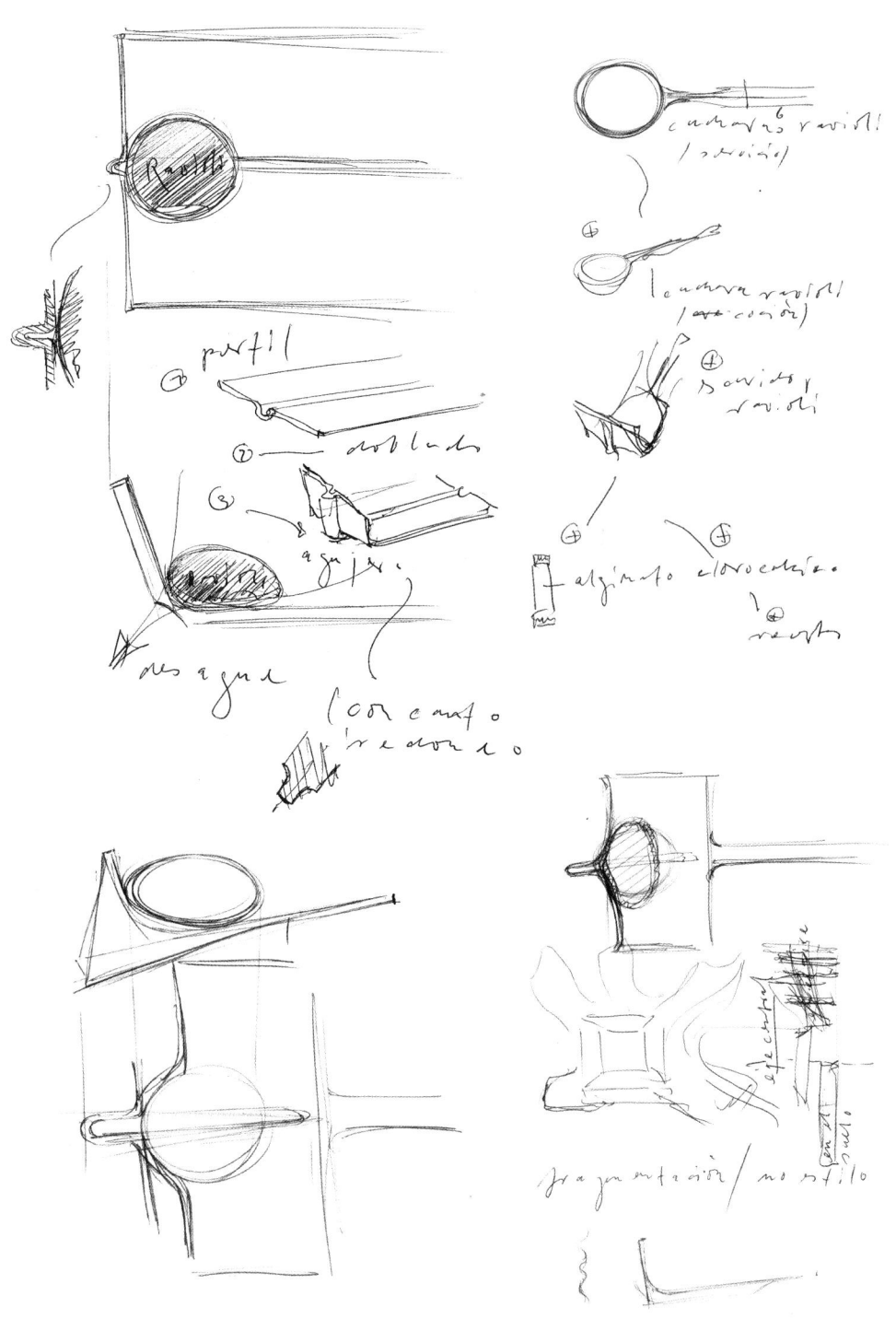

Marble spoon

This spoon was a response to the same challenge as that of the ravioli spoon, but of smaller size. It is a perfectly hemispherical spoon, also used to measure out medicine.

Marble spoon

⬛.. Idea for an industrial version

This design arose from a request by Jaume Biarnés, a chef at elBulli, who asked me for a spoon that could allow five spherical marbles to be made at a time with a single action. The result was this 'multiplier' spoon.

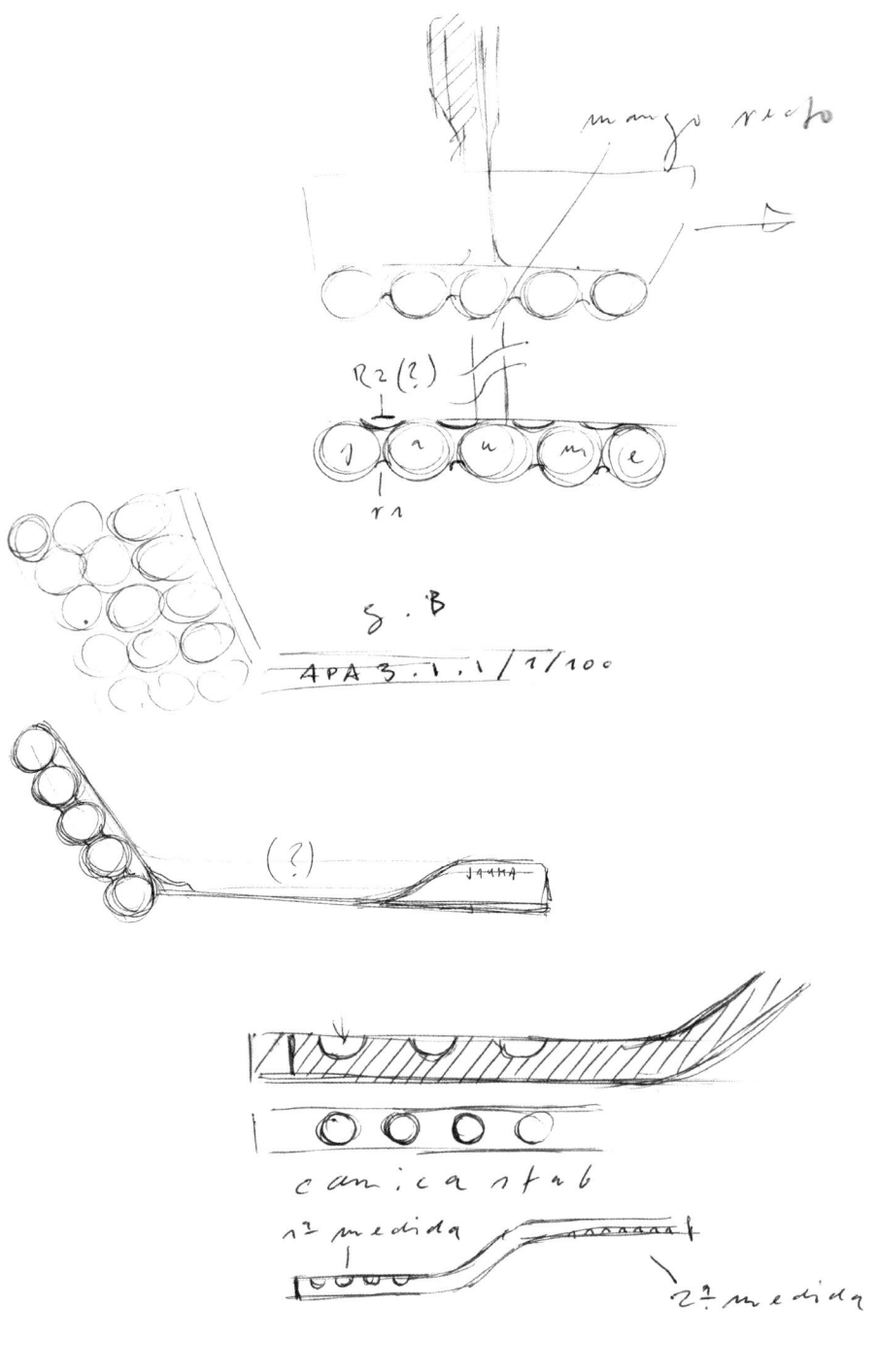

mango recto

R2(?)

1 1 u m e

r1

s . B

APA 3 . 1 . 1 / 1 / 100

(?)

JAMA

camic stab

1ª medida

2ª medida

Centrifuge

We were aware that we could respond to the hygiene demands of a kitchen by looking at laboratory equipment, so I went to the Expoquímica International chemistry show with the intention of finding things that could be used at elBulli.

Among the many things that piqued my curiosity were sheets of stainless steel mesh which were used in laboratories as sieves, which were later made into tableware. I also saw a distiller, the Rotaval, which we didn't see a use for at the time, but which later went on to be used for food preparation.

The main outcome of that visit was the centrifuge, with which glasses could be shaken at high speed so that the densest part of its contents would settle at the bottom.

I actually thought it could have been given greater use than it ended up having. The preparation that is synonymous with the centrifuge at elBulli was the tarragon concentrate, a 'drop' of intense flavour that was served on a concentrate spoon.

In the light of this and other similar experiences, I strongly recommend visiting trade shows that are unrelated to one's own industry, and I think it's a brilliant idea for extrapolating solutions from unrelated fields.

Spaghetto hose

I was already familiar with the flat jelly noodles dating from 1999. However, when I saw this hose two years later, I asked myself why we couldn't use it to make a *spaghetto*. First of all, the method was simple because the preparation was left to set in a tray and then cut into noodles.

But the *spaghetto* required the tubular shape that characterises this type of pasta, so what I did was to fill this PVC hose with Parmesan water in which agar-agar had been dissolved, which set as it cooled. This gave rise to our first jelly *spaghetto*. Now all we had to do was to take it out of the hose, but that's another story...

Candyfloss machine

One Christmas, there was a commercial on television for a candyfloss, a toy version of the machine you could see at a fairground. I thought it was a brilliant idea, and as it was important at elBulli to investigate new textures, I believed candyfloss could be a fantastic preparation.

Seeing that the machine was sold in Germany, I asked that it be sent to my parents in Switzerland, as they were planning to visit me in Barcelona. In fact, they brought five or six machines to me in Barcelona, because the toys weren't very reliable.

Once the interest in introducing this texture into elBulli was confirmed, we purchased a real candyfloss machine, identical to those found at fairgrounds, which allowed us to offer a new texture to the type of customer who wouldn't ordinarily go to a funfair, but who would reminisce about this surprising preparation.

Head for a candyfloss machine

🏭.. Idea for an industrial version

When we decided to use a candyfloss machine for making preparations at elBulli, we started out with a machine that had been sold as a toy, before moving onto a larger, professional machine. But I also experimented with creating our own design for the head.

I turned to a machine used in the laboratory, an electric stirrer with a rotating central shaft and a heating element. The task I set myself was to make a head that allowed the sugar to be introduced so that the candyfloss would exit through a groove.

The result had to be a candyfloss machine of suitable size for a restaurant. The intention was to design a commercial version, which explains the large number of sketches I made in relation to this project.

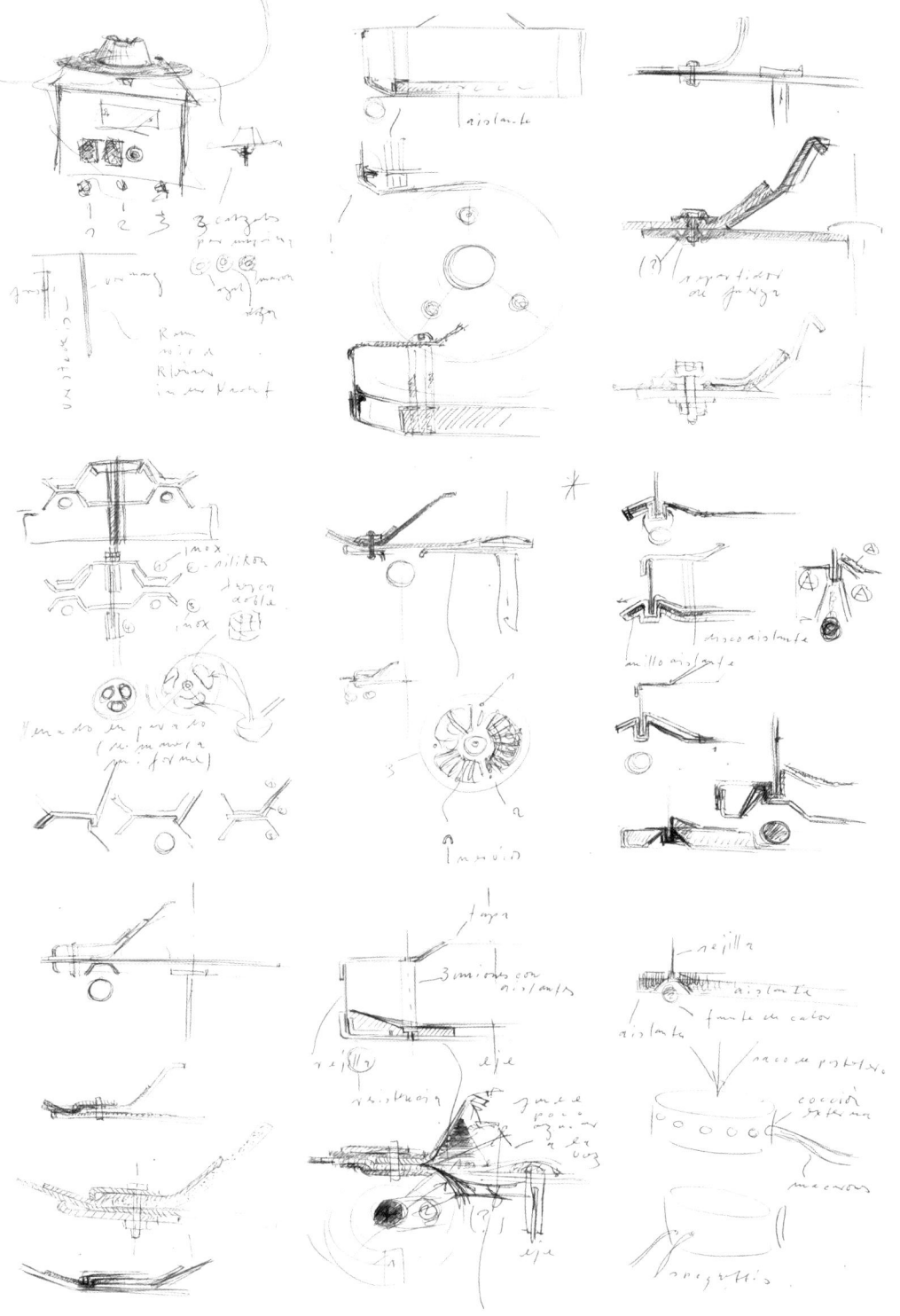

'Nitro-rotomoulding' with Kinder Surprise Egg

There is a technique in the world of industry known as rotational moulding or rotomoulding. It consists of a mould filled with plastic and rotated, causing the plastic to be deposited on the inner surface of the mould and take on its shape as it cools.

My idea was to reproduce this technique by filling a plastic 'Kinder Surprise Egg' with a liquid. The mould would then be immersed in liquid nitrogen in order to freeze. This was never put into practice in this form, but a version did appear in a way at elBulli in 2008, when I was no longer there, with balloons immersed in liquid nitrogen to create a giant Easter egg.

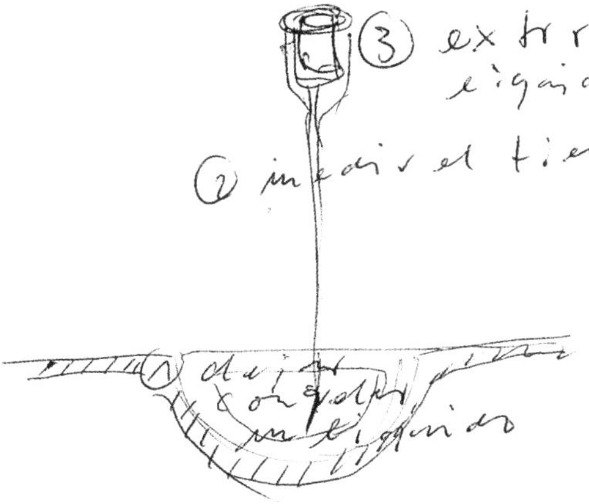

rollo
molde
en
frío

tirar
kinder
semi relleno
al
nitrógeno

y
girar

gorgueta - kinder
z.B. zumo de
zanahoria - color

Laser cutting and cooking

Laser cutting is used a great deal in industrial design. These sketches reflect two intentions. The first is to cut with precision, in other words, to be able to make exact portions. The second is to cook, given that a laser is a source of heat. For example, if we cut a tuna steak into cubes, the part closest to the cut will cook a little. This concept wasn't brought to fruition.

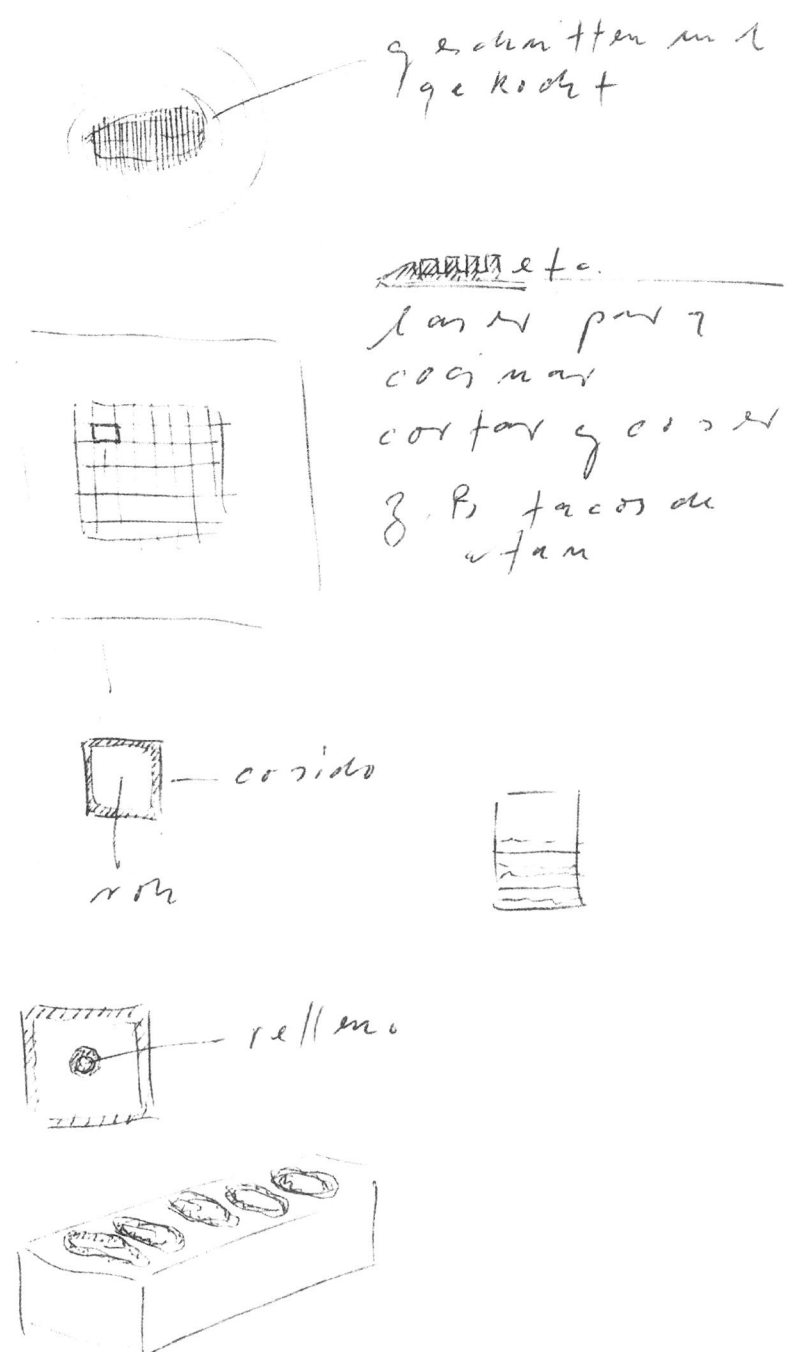

geschnitten und
gekocht

~~maqueta~~ eta.

laser para
cocinar
cortar y coser

8 R, tacos de
ufam

cosido

non

relleno

Laser setting

Taking advantage of the ability of directing the heat of a laser with great precision, we thought that we could use it to set certain preparations in a controlled manner. For instance, the white of an egg could be coagulated to form a sort of semolina at the points where the laser was applied. The result would be an egg white soup with dots of set egg white. It could also be applied to make strings. Like the previous idea, this one wasn't brought to fruition either.

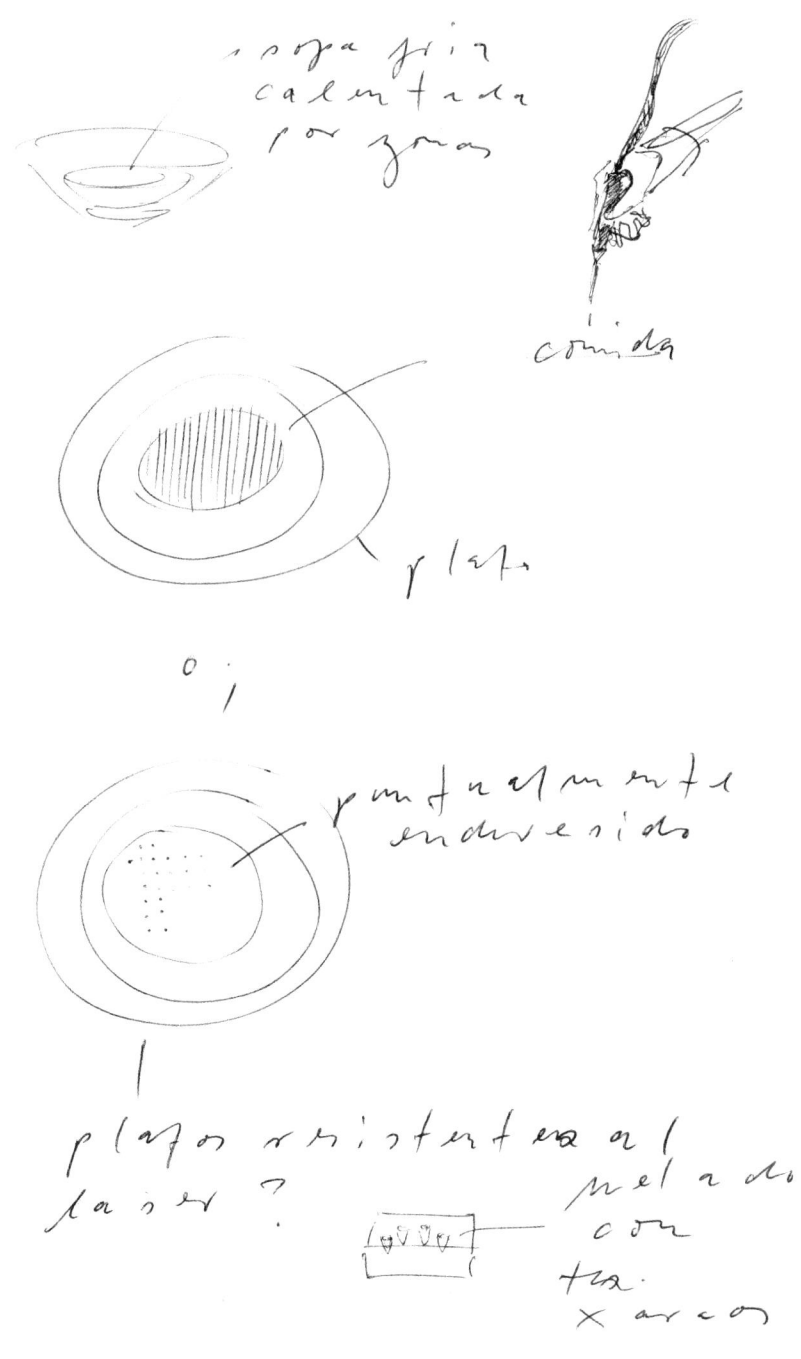

sopa fría
calentada
por zonas

comida

plato

o,

puntualmente
endurecido

platos resistentes al
laser?

melado
con
tra.
xarcos

Specifically designed objects for cooking

At certain times in the elBulli kitchen, very specific needs arose, particularly when new techniques appeared. For these cases, the necessary utensils or devices were often not to be found in the market, so we had to make them ourselves.

Before becoming a designer, I had learned the techniques of jewellery making; I knew how to file, cut, etc. In short, I could make items. In the world of product design, it's normal to make prototypes, and I could make small runs or have somebody else make them.

Adapter for siphon

Caviar maker

Synthesiser

THE SOUP moulds

Objects associated with liquid nitrogen

Adapter for caramel spring

Metal rod for making macaroni

Silicone moulds

Spaghetto nozzle

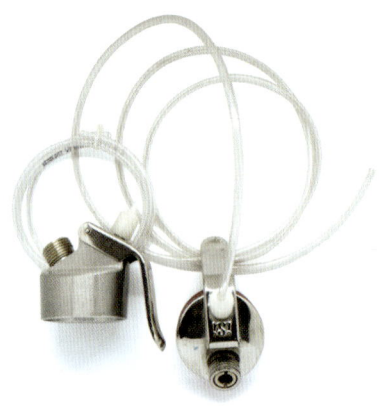

When making Parmesan water jelly *spaghetto* using PVC hose, we encountered a problem: how to remove the set *spaghetto* from the hose. It wasn't feasible to cut the PVC because the wall of the hose was thick and the *spaghetto* would be damaged, aside from not being able to reuse the hose.

I first attempted to inject air into the hose with a syringe, but because it contained so little air, I was only able to push out a very small part of the preparation. I later attempted to inject air using a bicycle pump, but this was cumbersome and not very hygienic. In the end, I built an adapter for a siphon. Because it used compressed air, it was easily able to expel the *spaghetto* from the hose.

In fact, it was quite a pleasing experience to see how it came out, and I heard that the process was performed in front of diners at 'special' tables.

Gnocchi nozzle

Once I'd discovered that I could make siphon nozzle adapters, I saw the possibility of creating new designs. At the time, around 2003, we conducted an experiment that lasted two days. Ferran told me to cook whatever I wanted from the perspective of a product designer.

This experiment actually failed, basically because I didn't dare touch the pantry without asking Oriol Castro for permission. Although he was very willing, he was also very busy with cooking tasks and couldn't spend the time I needed with me.

For example, one of the experiments that failed was an attempt to texturise a solid product with a high fat content, for which I asked Oriol to put a cube of foie gras into a siphon, but the result was completely unsatisfactory.

Despite these 'failures', a new dish did emerge. I conducted one experiment with a foam, adding sodium alginate to it and immersing a tube I'd designed for the siphon nozzle in a calcium chloride solution. The result was a spherical '*churro*' containing the foam. By cutting this *churro*, we obtained spherical gnocchi.

Gnocchi nozzle

.. Idea for an industrial version

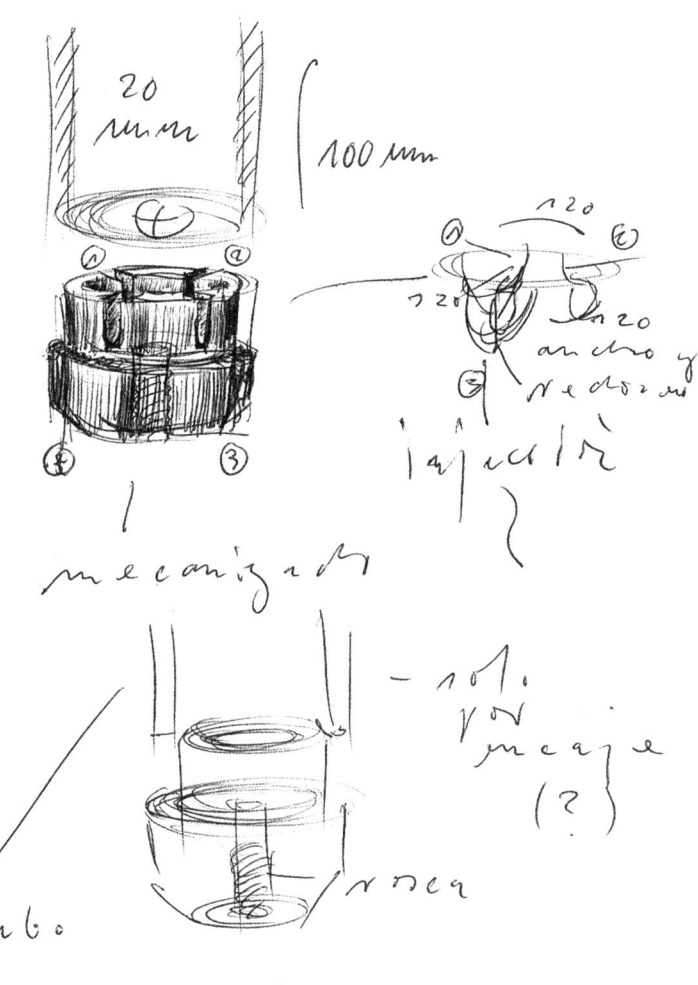

20
mm

100 mm

20

20
ancho y
redondo

inyector

20

mecanizado

rot.
por
encaje
(?)

tubo

rosca

Drop-by-drop – caviar maker

When Albert Adrià, after a visit to the Griffith company, discovered that caviar could be made from different products, one of the most famous elBulli techniques was born, spherification. The caviar was made using a syringe, by allowing a product to fall one drop at a time, in this case a melon juice containing sodium alginate, into a solution of calcium chloride. When the drop came into contact with the solution, a membrane was formed that encased the juice, leaving a ball with a liquid centre.

The spherification that was done in the early days greatly depended on the time the ball spent inside the solution, given that the membrane increasingly hardened until the entire ball became solid.

In other words, the time factor was crucial. But if you let a hundred drops fall into the solution, one at a time, the 'cooking time' of the first drop would be very different to that of the hundredth drop, given that the first would spend much more time inside the calcium chloride solution.

The solution was to make a bank of syringes by drilling a lot of holes into a board, each one holding a syringe. This way, a large number of drops would fall into the solution at the same time, standardising the cooking time for the caviar. At the same time, the *mise en place* could be done for the entire service, with the syringes filled and the caviar made as the time came for it to be served at each table.

Drop-by-drop for caviar made with two liquids

**.. Idea for an industrial version

This is a process for obtaining spheres containing one liquid inside, such as melon juice, with a membrane of another liquid, such as ham water.

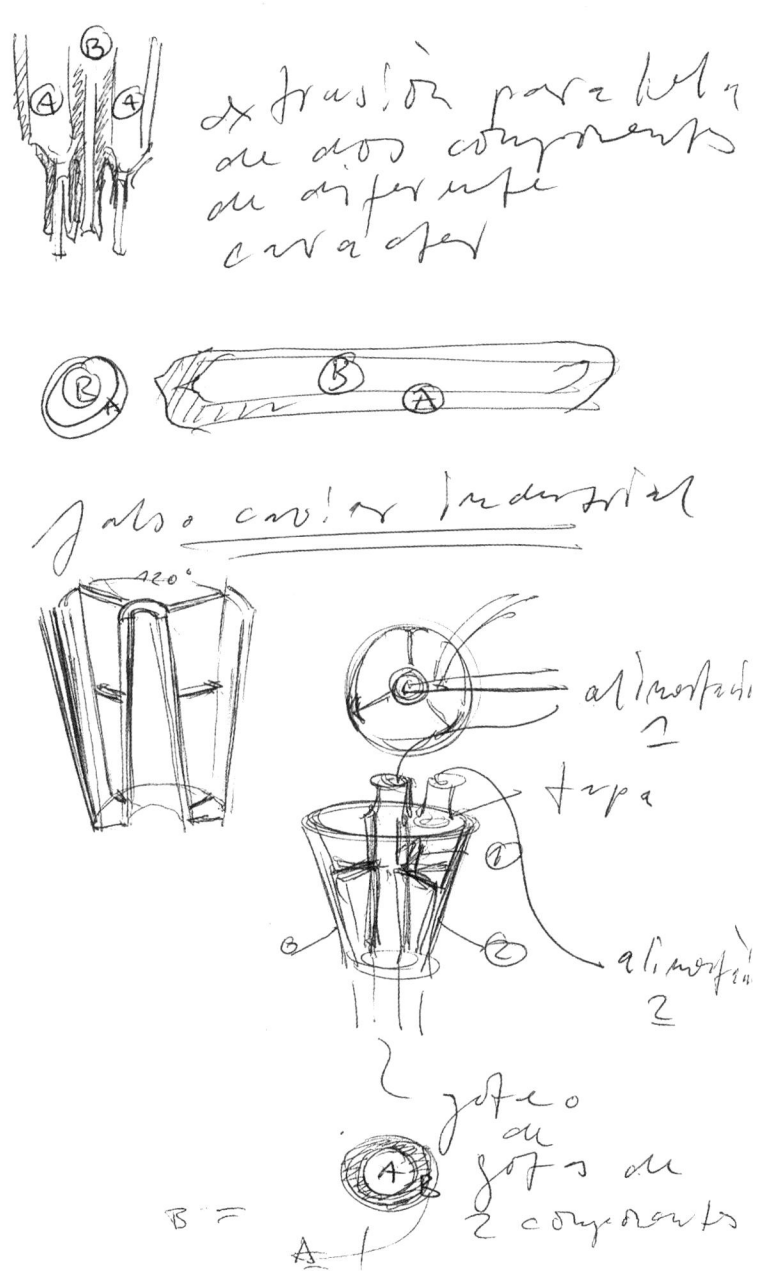

extrusión paralela
de dos componentes
de diferente
carácter

falso caviar Industrial

120°

alimentación
1

tapa

alimentación
2

goteo
de
gotas de
2 componentes

B =

A +

Aroma synthesiser

The aroma synthesiser was a response to the intention of serving an aroma to a diner at the same time as a preparation to be eaten. At the beginning, this was realised with the fantastic aromas created by Darío Sirerol, served as a spray.

Later, I tried out this machine, which came from the same supplier as the liquid nitrogen. It was filled with an aroma and closed. Then when the oxygen supply was switched on, a balloon was filled, containing the aroma.

THE SOUP moulds

This mould reflected Albert Adrià's desire to create a pop version of an alphabet soup. For this purpose, I turned to a baking supplies shop and had moulds specially made to spell out the letters of THE SOUP, which would form part of a dessert that was actually a soup.

Air-baguette

When the idea of making *air-baguettes* came about, we found we needed a mould that would allow us to make exact replicas. For this, we turned to the same baking supplies shop where we had gone for other equipment, such as the moulds for THE SOUP, for instance. There I had this mould specially made which included a handle, providing precise and easy cutting.

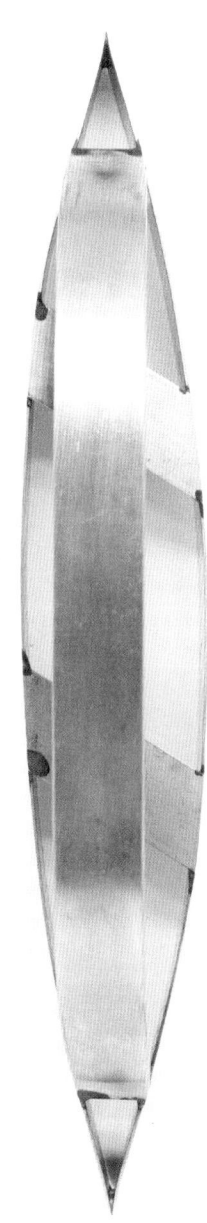

Inter-tine mould for a fork

The idea was to make a mould using the same technology that went into the moulds for THE SOUP.

With this mould, we would be able to make an 'inter-tine' preparation, i.e., something with projecting parts that would fit between the tines of a fork. If a fork had four tines, for instance, you would be able to fill up to three inter-tine spaces. I always thought that it would be interesting to have the inter-tine fillings made of different flavours and/ or textures.

However, the preparation would not be able to touch the surface on which the fork was resting.

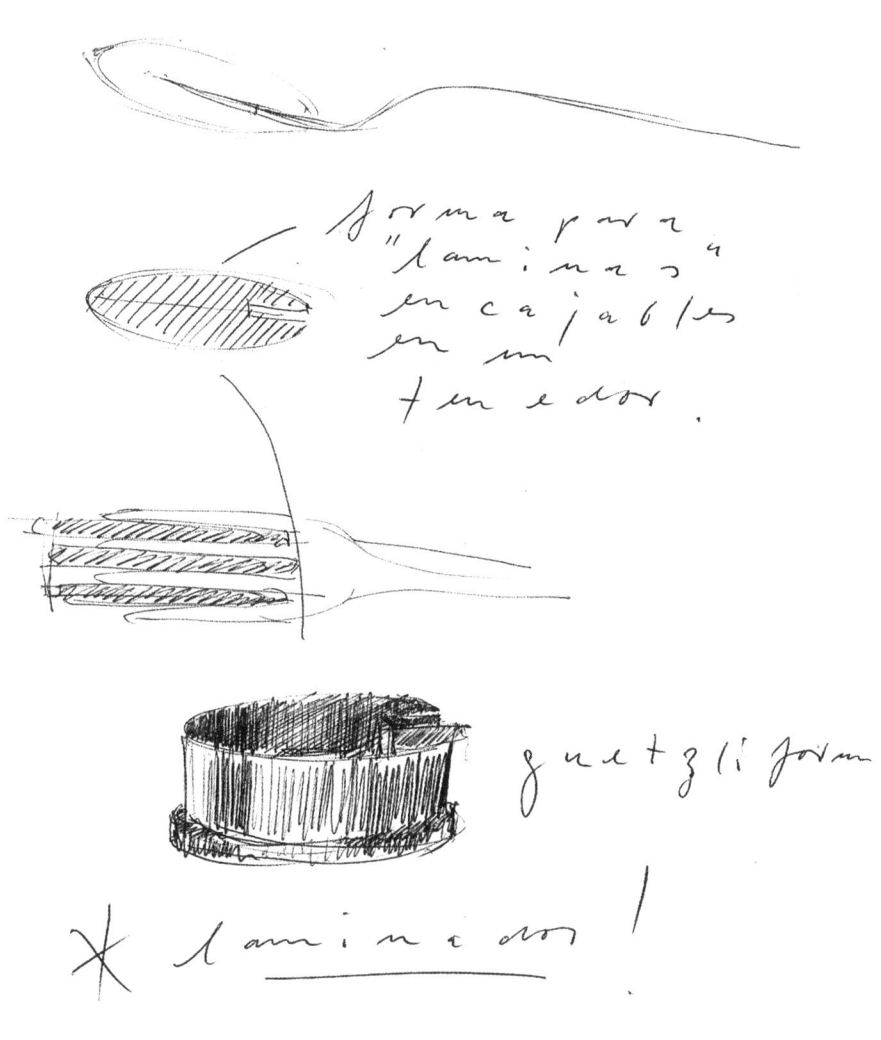

forma para
"laminas"
encajables
en un
tenedor.

guetzli form

✳ laminados !

Nitrogen bowl

Nitrogen in a liquid state has a temperature of -192°C, which means that handling it is as dangerous or even more dangerous than working with fire. If poured into a uninsulated bowl, it would be impossible to pick it up with your hands without 'burning' them. It could also be dangerous for patrons if the bowl were to be used at the table.

This is why we worked with Cunill to create a bowl with a double chamber. It consisted of metal exterior, another piece of metal to form the hemispherical interior, and a nylon disc between both parts to provide maximum insulation.

Nitro-marble spoon

By taking a spoon for making spherical marbles and adding insulation against the extremely low temperatures of liquid nitrogen, we thought of immersing the convex part of a very cold spoon into a liquid so that it would freeze.

* nitrógeno líquido ;
bañar herramientas
en nitrógeno líquido
para ;

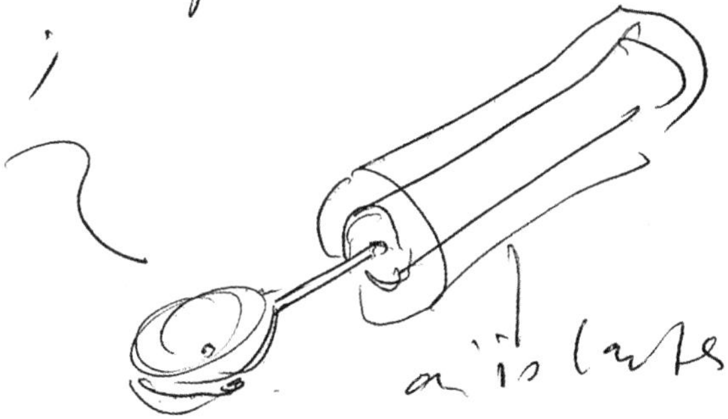

Nitro moulds

These moulds are inspired by a traditional method from Valencia, which consists of dipping a mould into batter and plunging it into boiling oil. The team at elBulli thought that this method could work using liquid nitrogen, and that these moulds could make it happen.

In fact, any thermoconducting object with a shape that allows a preparation to be easily unmoulded (e.g. with a conical or more or less spherical shape) could serve this purpose, such as spoons, door knobs and bowls.

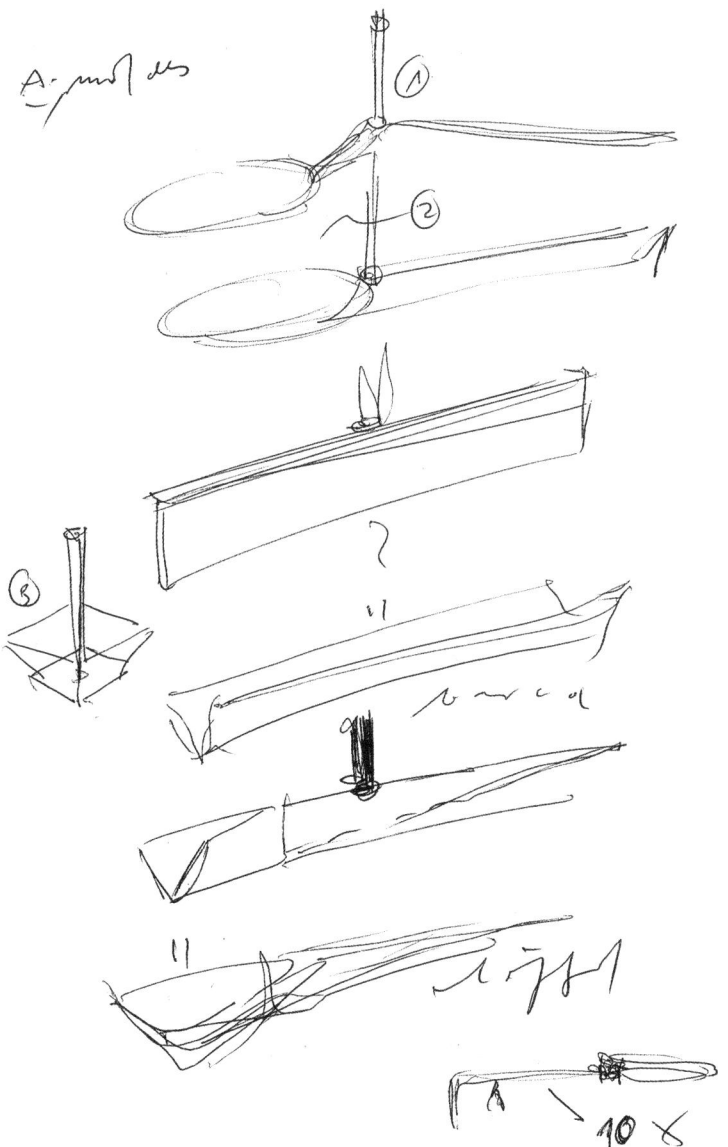

'Nitro-teppan'

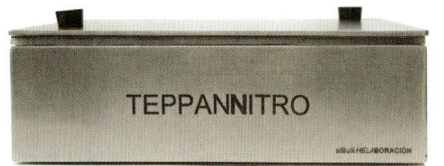

This design came about when liquid nitrogen began to be used at elBulli. The intention was to make something resembling a *teppan*, a Japanese griddle, but which made use of cold instead of heat. We achieved this by constructing a receptacle with a double chamber so that there was no risk for either diners or waiters. The liquid nitrogen was poured into this receptacle so that thermoconducting panels inside – like those of a radiator – would receive the cold, allowing it to reach the surface of the griddle. This is how we created a cold griddle on which frozen preparations could be made instantly, mostly in front of diners.

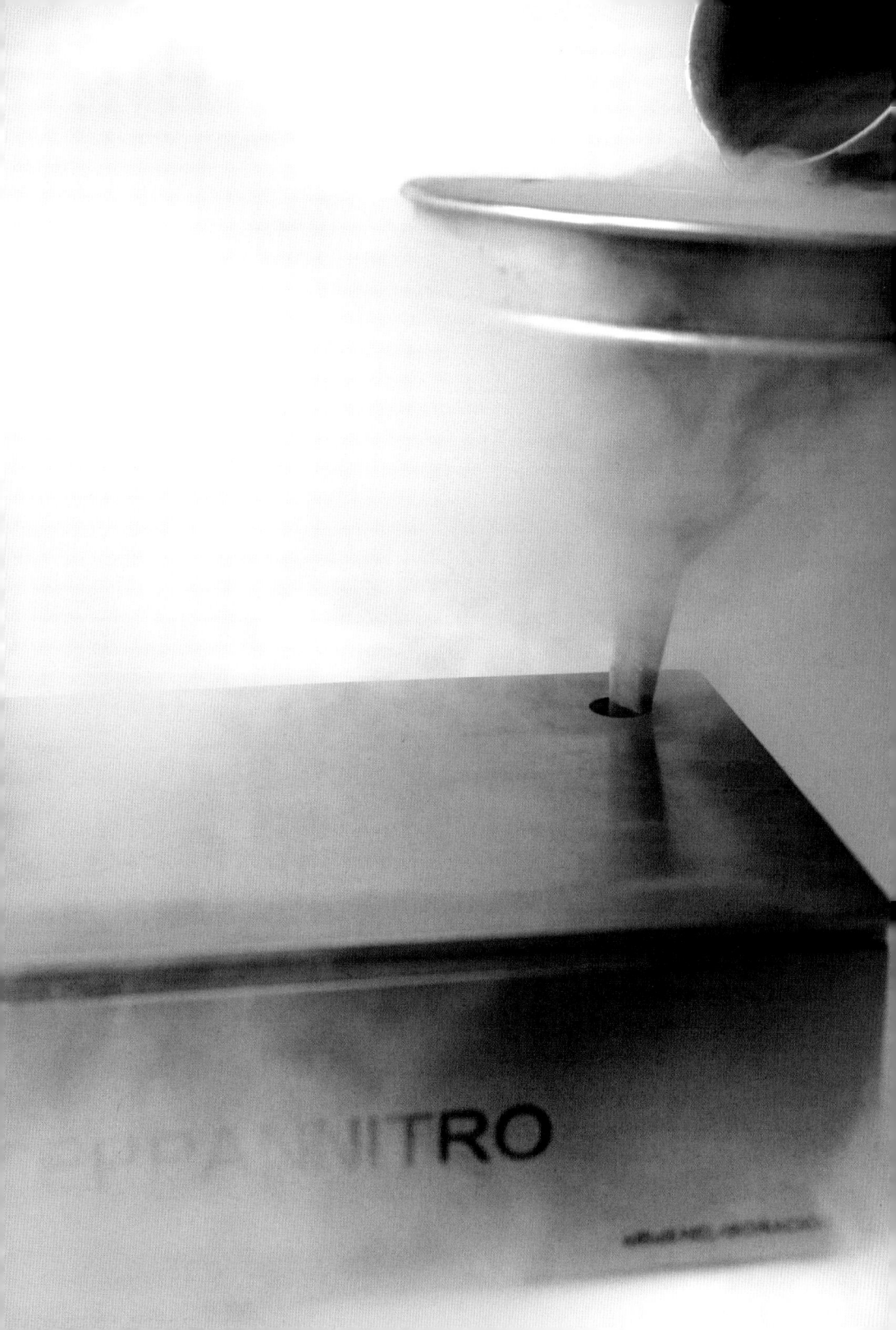

'Nitro-teppan'

Adapter for caramel spring

The olive oil caramel spring was a magical preparation that resembled a ring. In order to make it, caramel was heated under a sugar lamp and kept at a consistency that would allow it to be worked. Albert had realised that a very fine thread could be made with a very pretty sheen. An attempt was made to roll it by hand, but it was a very laborious process. We then took an electric screwdriver, and I created this adapter with a slight taper, allowing the spring to be easily removed. Despite this, the spring was extremely fragile, and it would often break. For this reason, and because it resembled a ring, we served it in a jewellery box.

Adapter for caramel spring

fallos ≠ fallas
= almacén

MEN   APA   ETC

pizarra

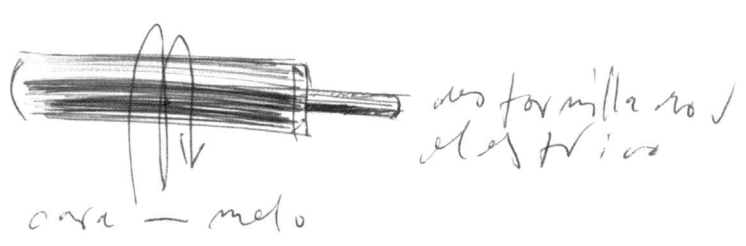

destornillador
eléctrico

cera — meto

remache

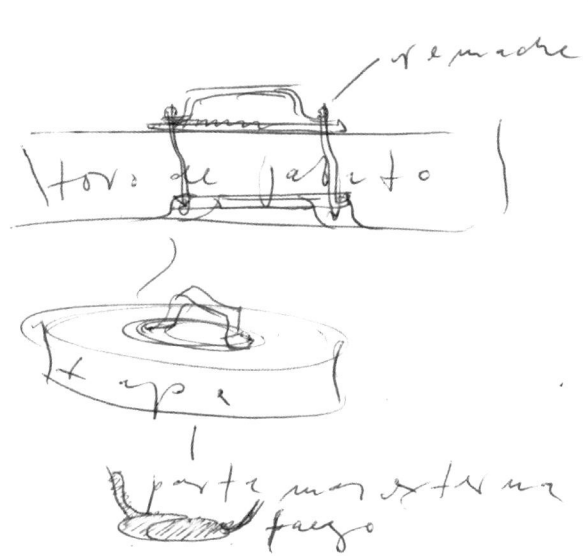

foro de labeto

tapa

parte mas externa
fuego

Metal rod for making macaroni

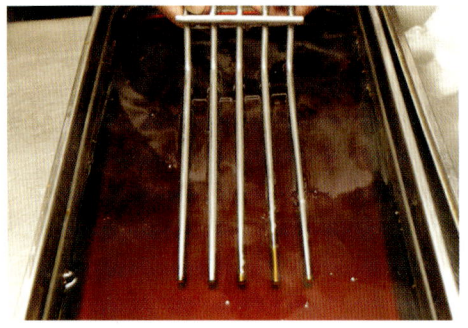

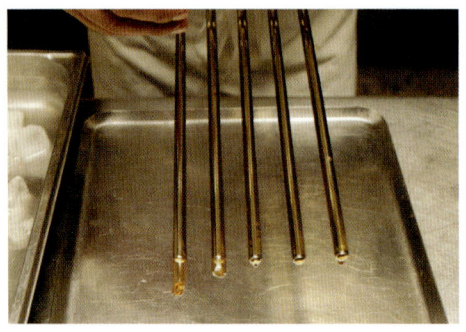

This consisted of dipping a metal rod in jelly, letting the part adhering to the rod set, and later sliding it off, creating a long tube that was cut on the diagonal to resemble macaroni. The final design was a series of rods, allowing several tubes to be formed at the same time.

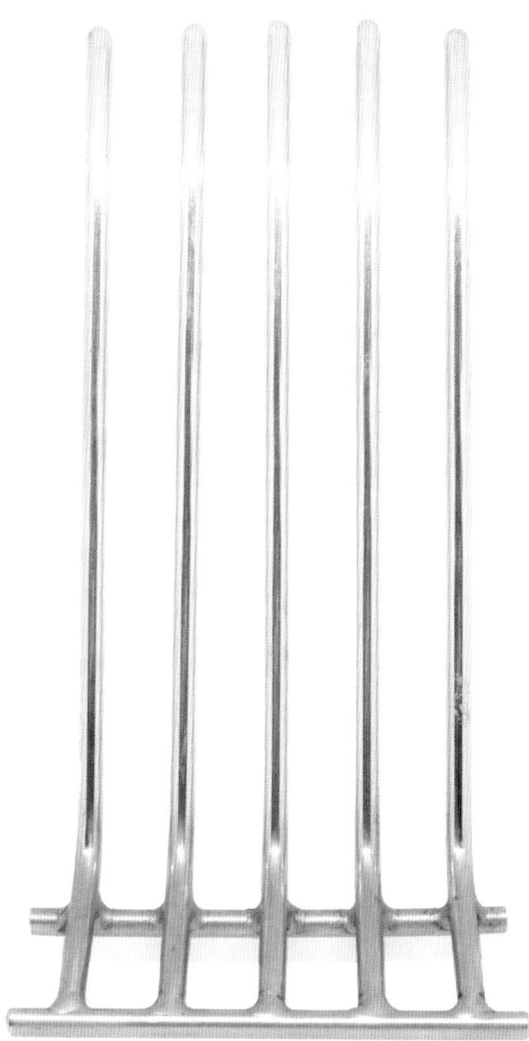

Metal rod for making macaroni

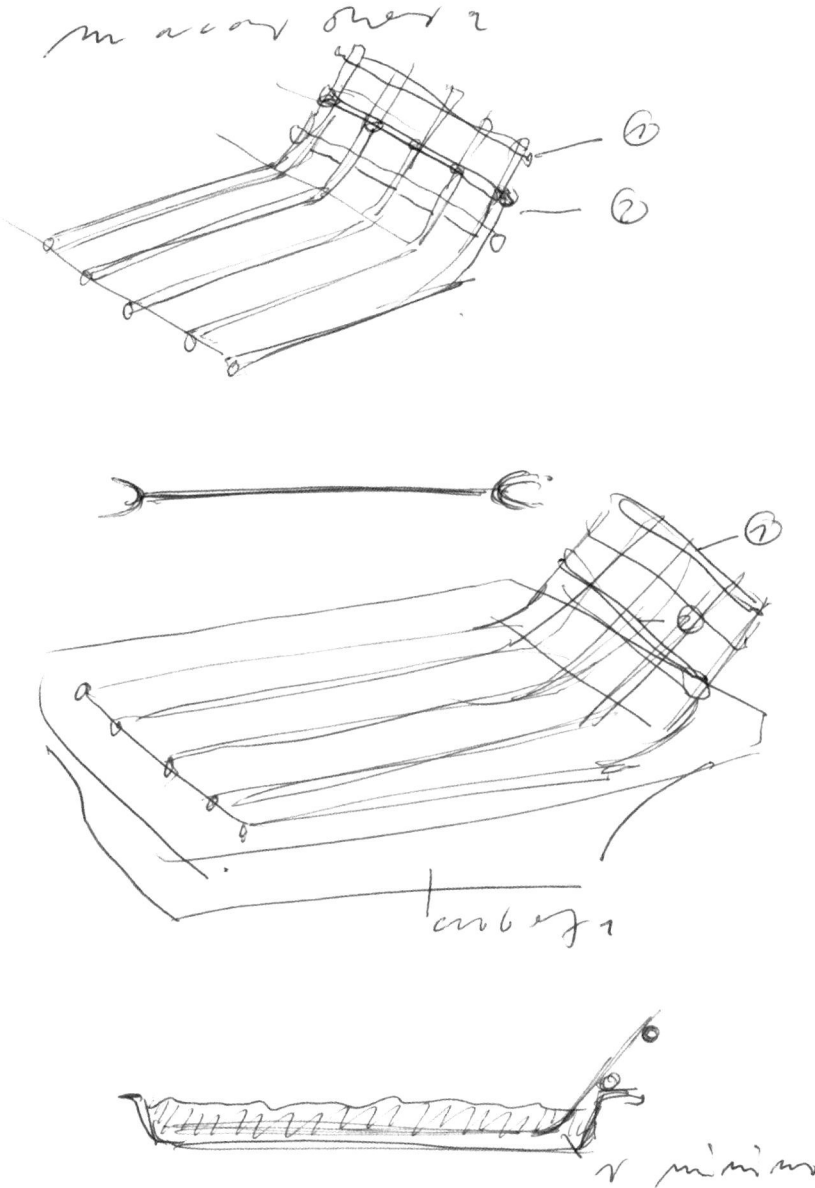

Spaghettini needle

The initial brief for this design was to use a needle and syringe for cooking, with a view to the extremely fine product that could be ejected from it. It wasn't used in the time I was at elBulli, but it was later turned to in order to make *spaghettini*.

(jKuh lebt noch!)

Blut

Wurst

pfanne mit Butter

oder ofen   Feuer   (natur)

Silicone moulds

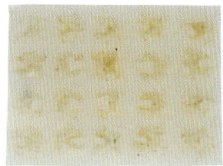

Among the materials we had at our disposal was silicone, which was made by mixing two components, a liquid and a catalyst. This procedure allowed moulds and shapes of all kinds to be obtained. The first moulds we made were the result of the intention of mimicking different sorts of food, and these were later put to good use at elBulli. Other examples were a dessert by Albert Adrià called Moon, which replicated a footprint on the surface of the moon, and moulds for chocolates with which we tried to imitate botanical drawings.

Shot mould

The intention in this case was to make a silicone mould to obtain perfect spheres, for which we experimented with real shot pellets.

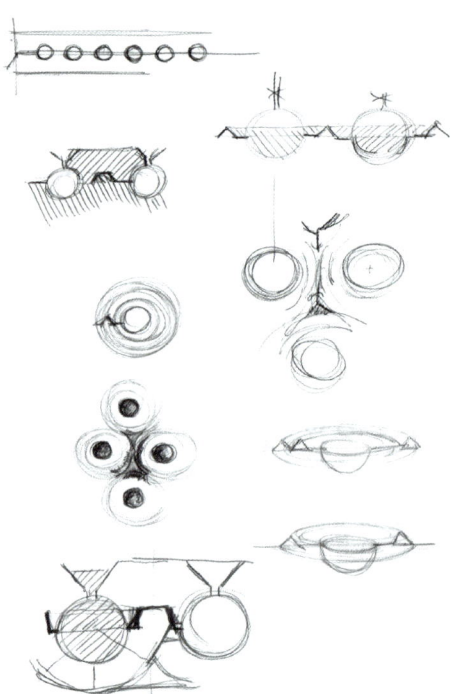

Mould for frozen ravioli

Following on from the concept of the frozen pastille, I thought that we could make ravioli (i.e. a filled preparation) by creating a mould with the same shape as the pastille, but hollow. In order to make a raviolo, two of these moulds would have to be joined together around a filling.

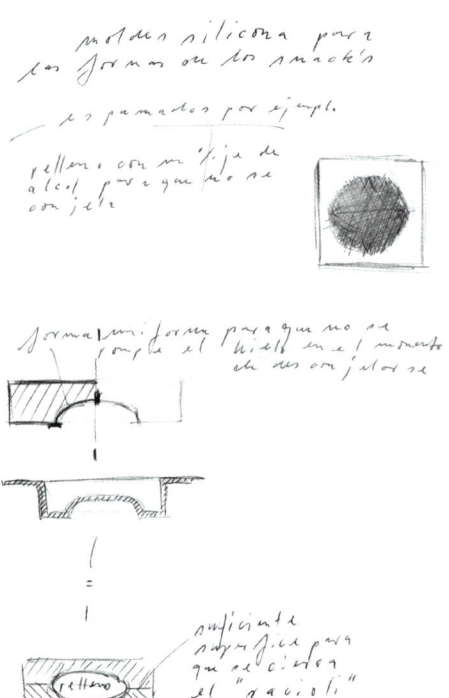

Moulds to imitate edible shapes

My favourite dish is my grandmother's green beans with bacon, which is a childhood memory. The idea here was to make a mould that could be filled with a bean and bacon preparation in the shape of a green bean.

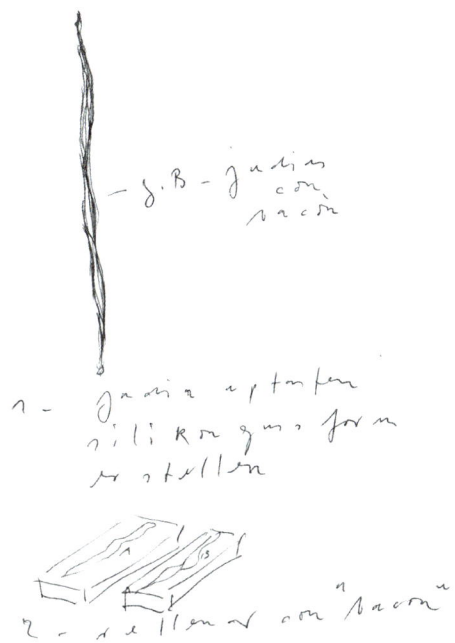

Atomiser nozzle for siphon

Spray bottles are something we see very often, for example with cleaning products. They are able to atomise liquids, but not products such as oil. The surface density of oil is too high, so when the spray mechanism is activated, what comes out is a thin stream.

What came to mind was to apply pressure by using a siphon, which could allow oils to be sprayed. Taking advantage of the relationship between Ferran and the ISI company, I was interested in designing a specific nozzle that could be commercialised together with the siphon.

This is the other version of the siphon atomiser nozzle, with more of a home-made feel. It didn't get past the drawing stage, but I think I would be able to make it today.

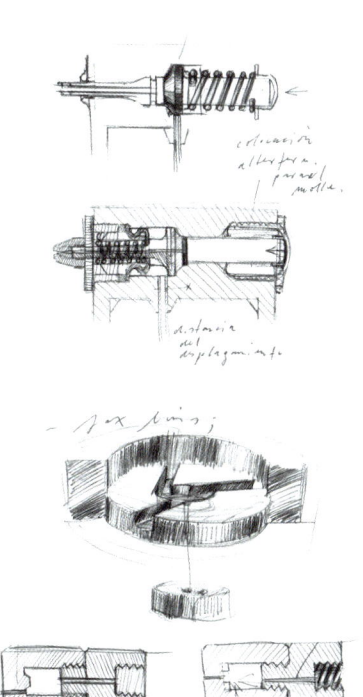

'Blöterle'
(the Swiss German word for blowing bubbles with a straw)

'Don't play with your food!' This is what millions of parents have told their children on countless occasions. It is used, for instance, when children blow through a straw to make bubbles in their drink, an action which is called *Blöterle* in Swiss German. 'You mustn't do that!' How many times have we heard this said, when it is actually a fun thing to do.

It is also fun to think that what happened most of the time at elBulli was exactly that, playing with food. To give an example, the act of blowing bubbles through a straw is the principle of the elBulli airs, which were made by whipping the surface of a liquid to create bubbles.

In our case, we wanted to reproduce this effect using the *spaghetto* adapter, by inserting a PVC hose into a glass and imitating this typical childhood action.

blóferle

sifón

blóferle legítimo

'Blöterle' - helium

This is a new version of the bubbles, but using helium. We wanted to achieve this using an air cylinder, by introducing a tube into a liquid and adding helium, in order for the bubbles to float away.

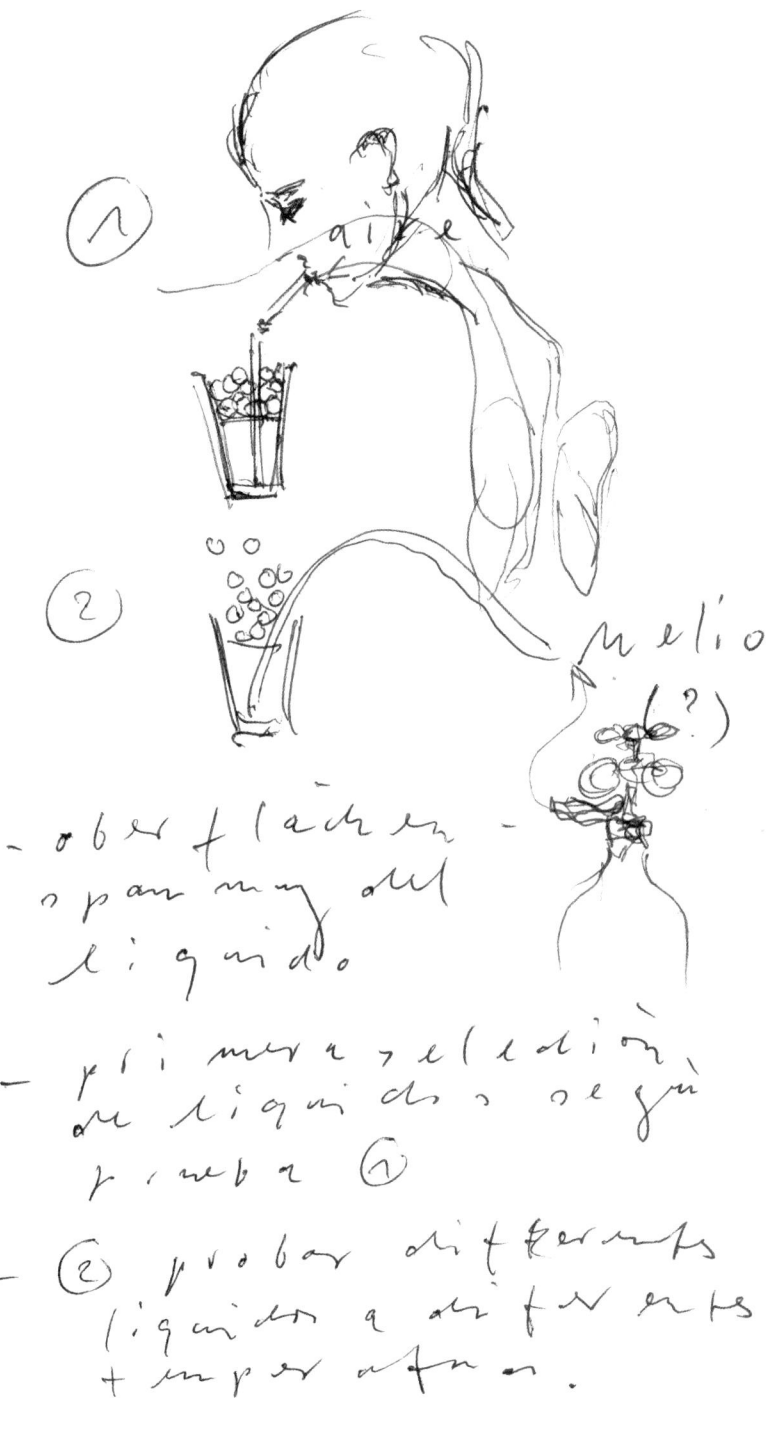

Air synthesiser

I also considered making bubbles by means of a synthesiser, by positioning a tiny, very closely woven mesh at one end, so that very small bubbles would appear when air was applied.

To do this I attached the *spaghetto* hose adapter to the siphon with this 'reducer' at the outlet. I tested out different diameters to see if this variation affected the bubbles, but I saw that the size didn't depend on the diameter, but on the composition of the liquid, amount of air, etc.

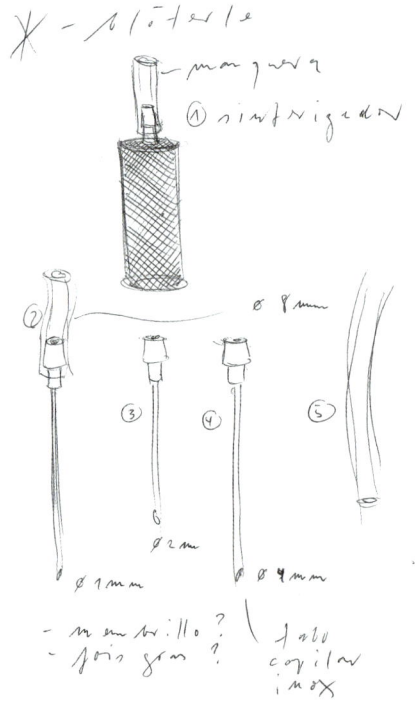

Helium synthesiser

This is a new version using helium, with an inlet for the siphon and another for this gas.

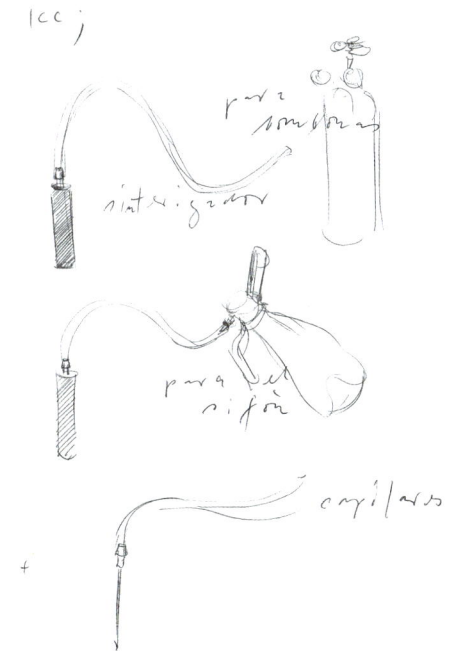

Eclipse nozzle

This is a progression on the method for making bubbles, with the addition of a propeller-shaped attachment to whip the liquid. The idea was to make a propeller with hoses that would direct the air from the siphon to make the blades turn.

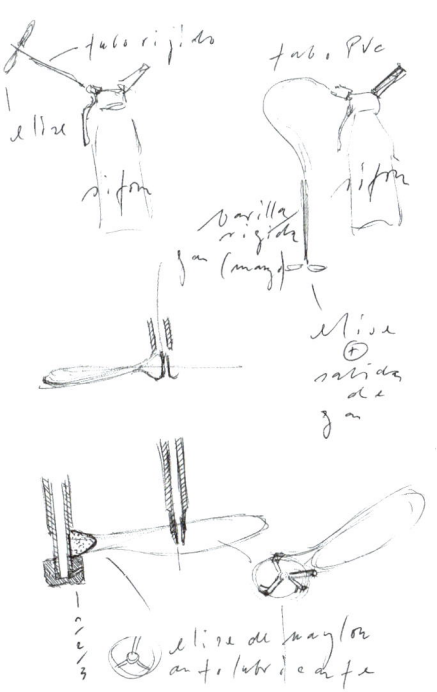

Drop-by-drop
for spherical marbles

The intention of this drop-by-drop device
was to make something similar to the
caviar maker but with the size of spherical
marbles.

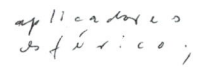

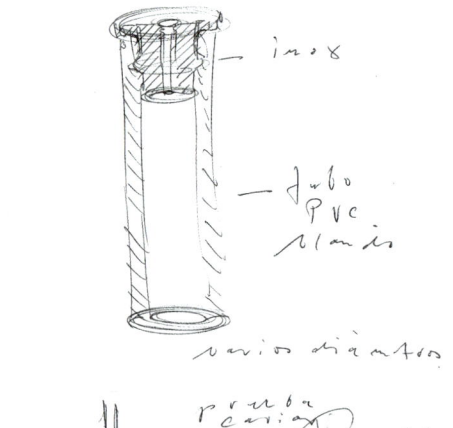

'Helium-gnocchi' nozzle

Could we achieve a texture even lighter
than that of air by using helium in the
texturising process?

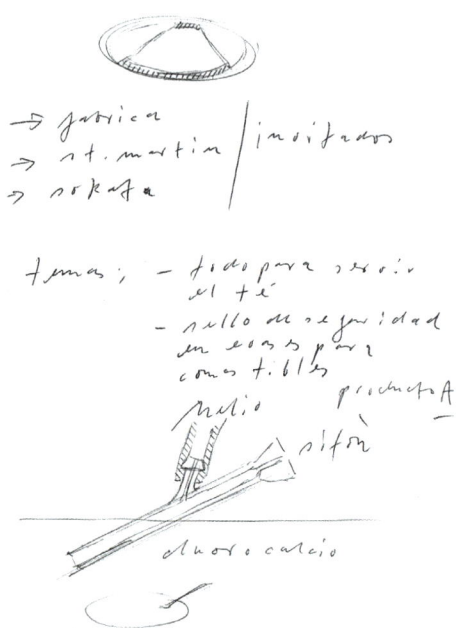

Caviar drip feeder

💼.. Idea for an industrial version

This was the other alternative to the bank of syringes for the production of spherical caviar. This feeder works by having the liquid mixed with sodium alginate come down the tube and drip through a number of holes into the calcium chloride solution.

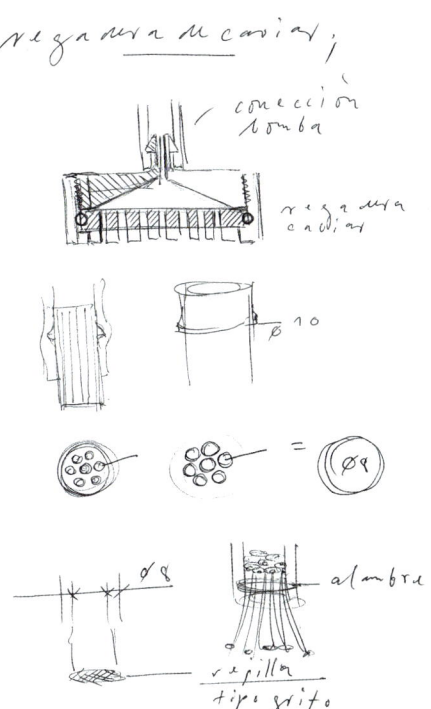

Gnocchi adapter

Sketch for the industrial version of the gnocchi adapter.

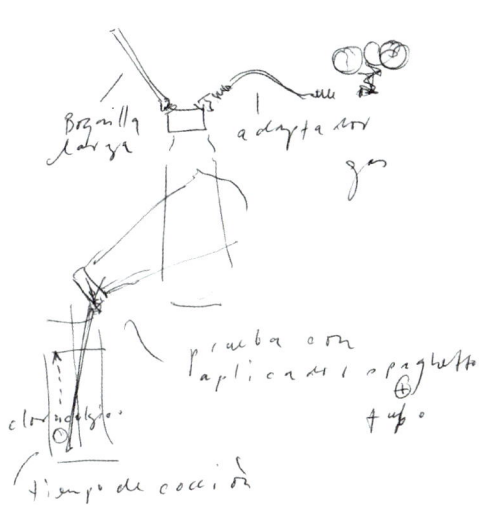

1–3 Shot mould

4–6 Blown sugar mould

7   Product imitation silicone mould
8   Drilled moulds
9   Frozen mould

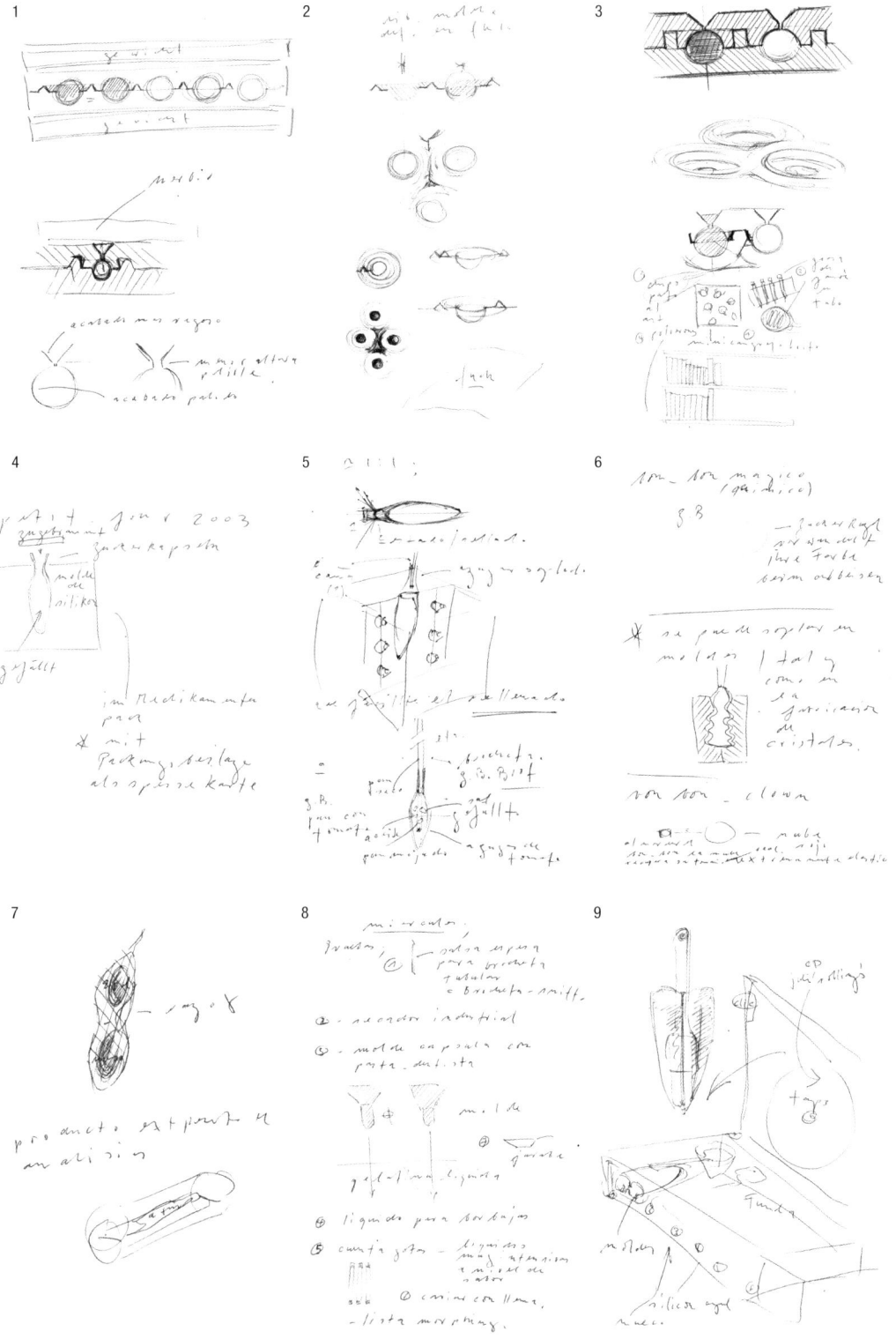

1 Spatulas
2 Adapter for siphon
3 Adapter for filling marrow skewer

4 Loaf tin
5 Siphon nozzle
6 Nozzles

7 Croquanter
8 Nitro moulds
9 Croquette + ravioli spoons

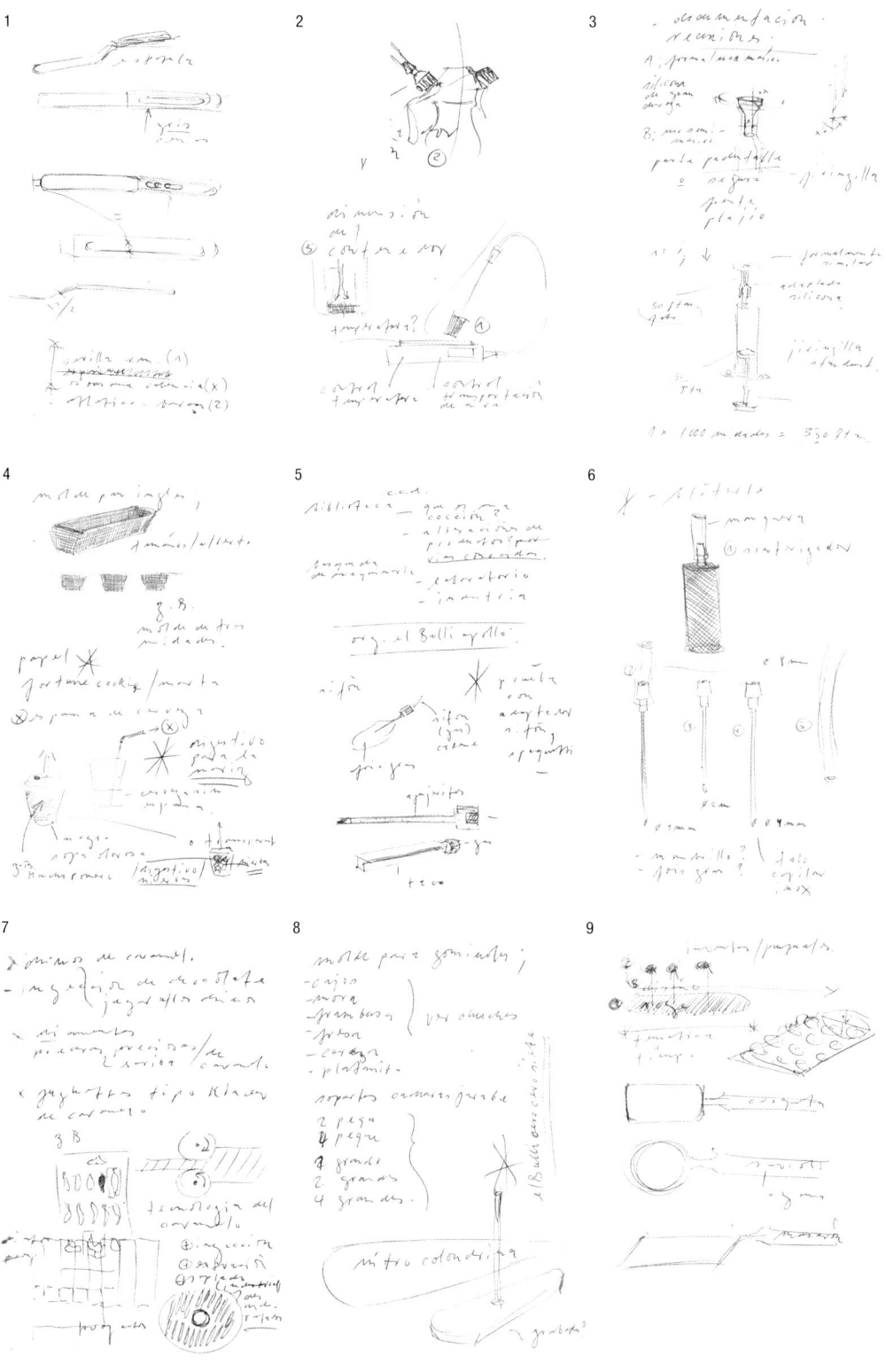

Other sketchbook notes

This section includes everything I thought up or drew that wasn't directly related to my main activity at elBulli. Many of the sketches reflect my desire, which I've already explained, of transcending the utility of the objects for the restaurant and to make possible their mass production.

Others are related activities in parallel with those at elBulli in which I was given the opportunity to participate. Finally, there are other more personal notes, the result of the personal nature of the sketchbooks, which accompanied me throughout this collaboration.

Iced coffee set

Because Ferran had entered into a collaboration agreement with Lavazza, which still endures, we wanted to design a set for making iced coffee that would allow two receptacles to be used like a cocktail shaker.

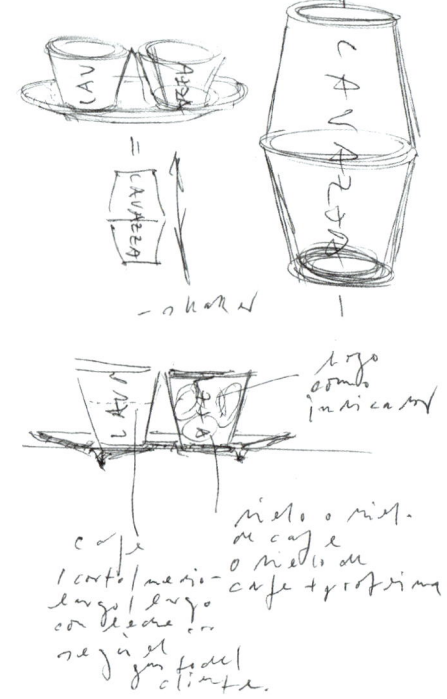

Catering pipettes

Single-use pipettes designed for catering, previously filled with sauce.

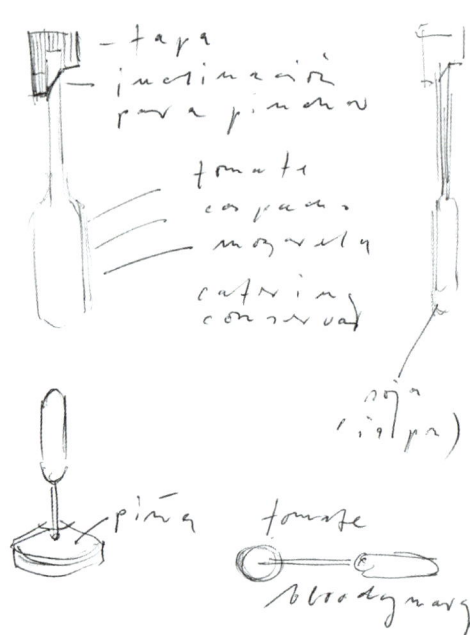

294

Coffee shaker pack

A commercial packaging design allowing coffee to be shaken to produce a frothy consistency.

Chupa-Chup with sniff or pipette

This is a concept thought up for retail, consisting of a Chupa-Chup-style lollipop combined with a sniff or pipette filled with sauce, Pop Rocks or pellets of a certain product or preparation, among others.

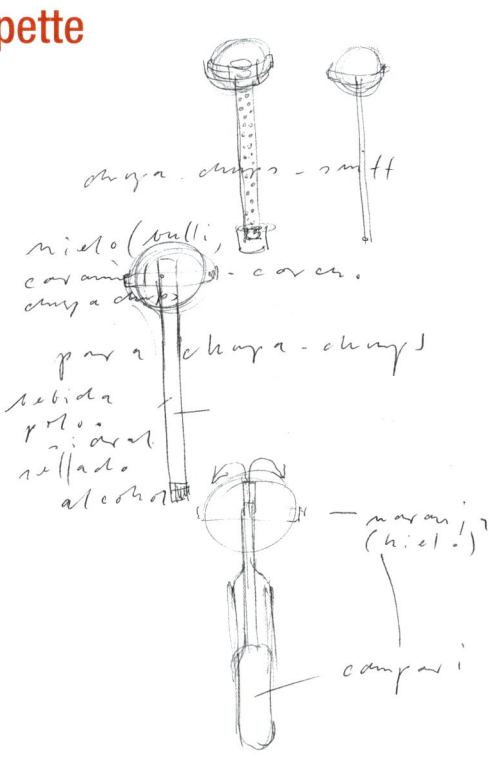

Pack for making ice cubes

This design was created with retail in mind.
It was about making ice trays filled with
mineral water for sale in supermarkets.
They would be sealed in clear plastic and
the brand of water printed on the package.

The idea is to be able to purchase this ice
tray, put it into the freezer and make quality
ice cubes of the desired brand of water. It is
merely another way of selling water.

I also came up with a version in a Tetra Brik,
in the shape of an inverted triangle.

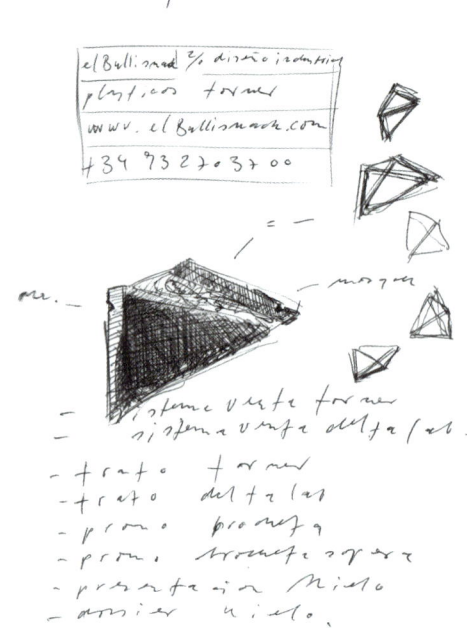

Packaging for two separated components

A commercial concept that could
be applied to a medication: the two
components are sealed separately, and
when the packaging is broken, they are
mixed.

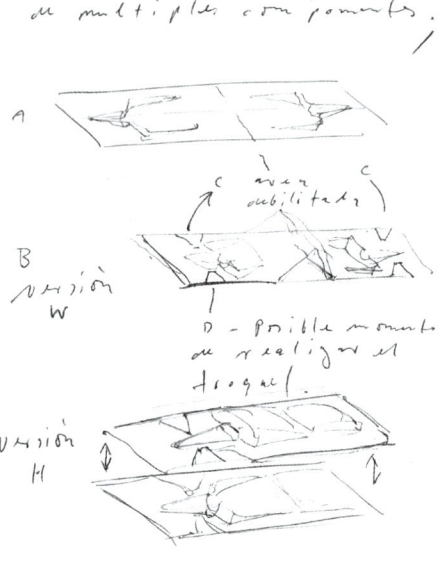

Puppet packaging

An idea for baby food. The package
is a round bowl filled with baby food,
with a hole in the middle. There is a soft
figure in the hole which can be turned
into a finger puppet to keep baby
entertained while eating.

Packaging with dropper
for salad dressings

This was created for the Borges company,
with which Ferran was collaborating.

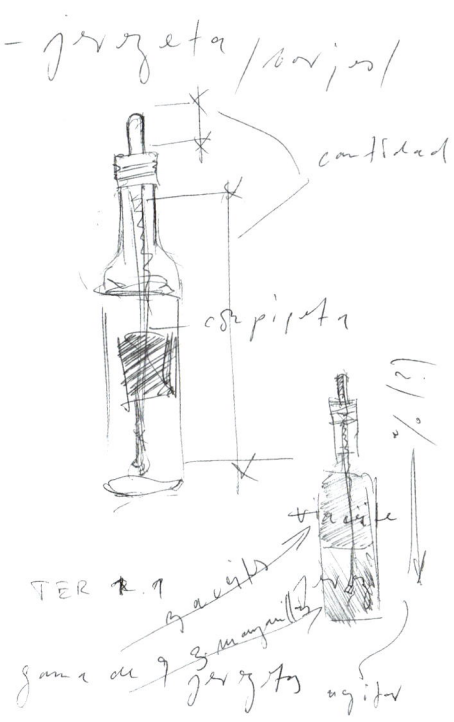

Microwaveable moka pot

The moka pot is an icon of Italian design
known throughout the world. In order for
it to be used in a microwave, its materials
need to be changed.

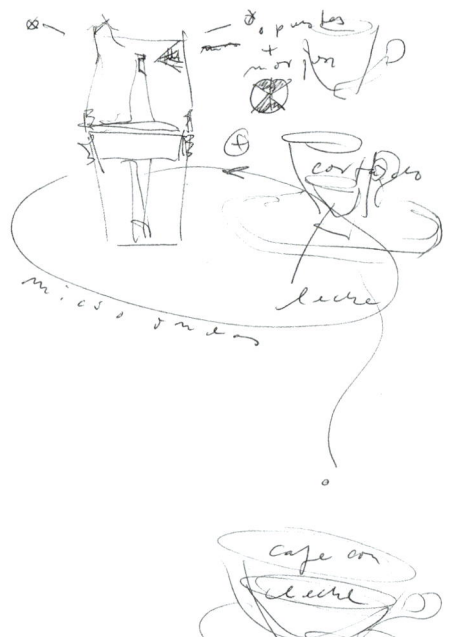

Ultrasonic cleaner

Ultrasound is commonly used for cleaning
jewellery. The item to be cleaned is
immersed in a liquid with a little soap and
the ultrasound eliminates the dirt from areas
of chains and other items that are difficult
to reach. Dentists also use ultrasound on
items that are difficult to clean. In this case,
we wanted to make use of it for kitchen
hygiene.

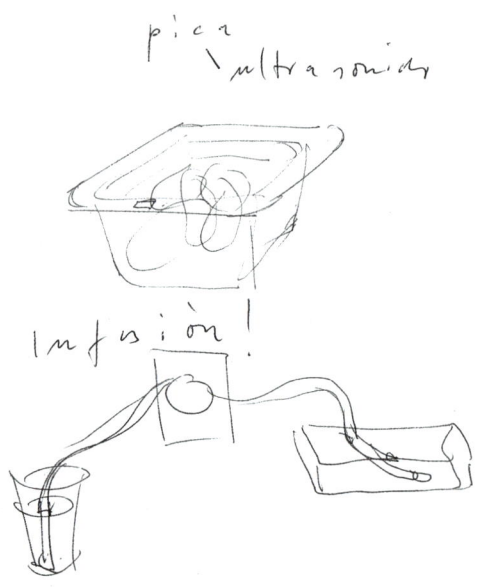

Coffee machine for water bottle

A design consisting of a small coffee machine that is attached to a water dispenser refill bottle. When the water runs out, the coffee machine is transferred to another bottle.

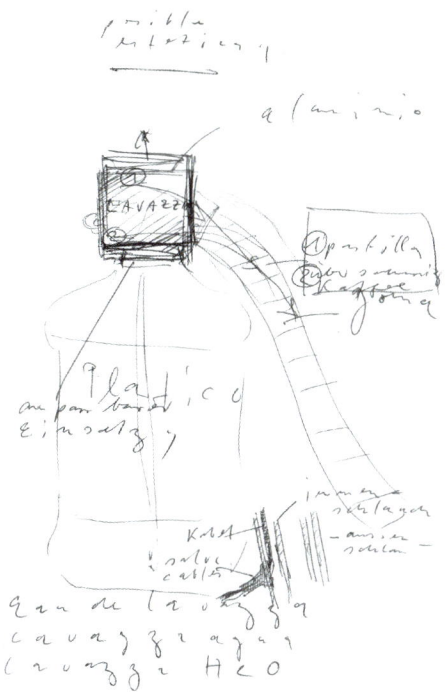

Gilding film for microwave oven

Gilding can't be done in a microwave oven, only heating and, with certain foods, cooking. Nor can you use any metallic objects. But if this fact is turned on its head, then the sparks can be used to apply gold leaf to a product.

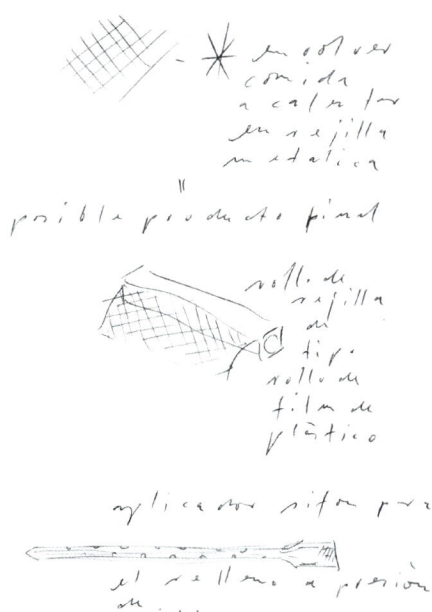

Vinaigrette spoon

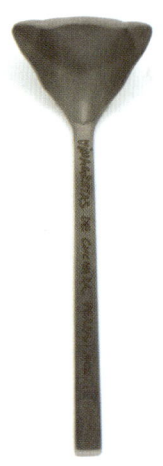

This spoon with the shape of a small bull was meant to be a reflection of the bull figurine in the elBulli kitchen. This is a promotional version for Borges, a company with which Ferran had an agreement. The idea was that it could be used to serve vinaigrette, regardless of whether the user was right-handed or left-handed, using one or the other horn to pour.

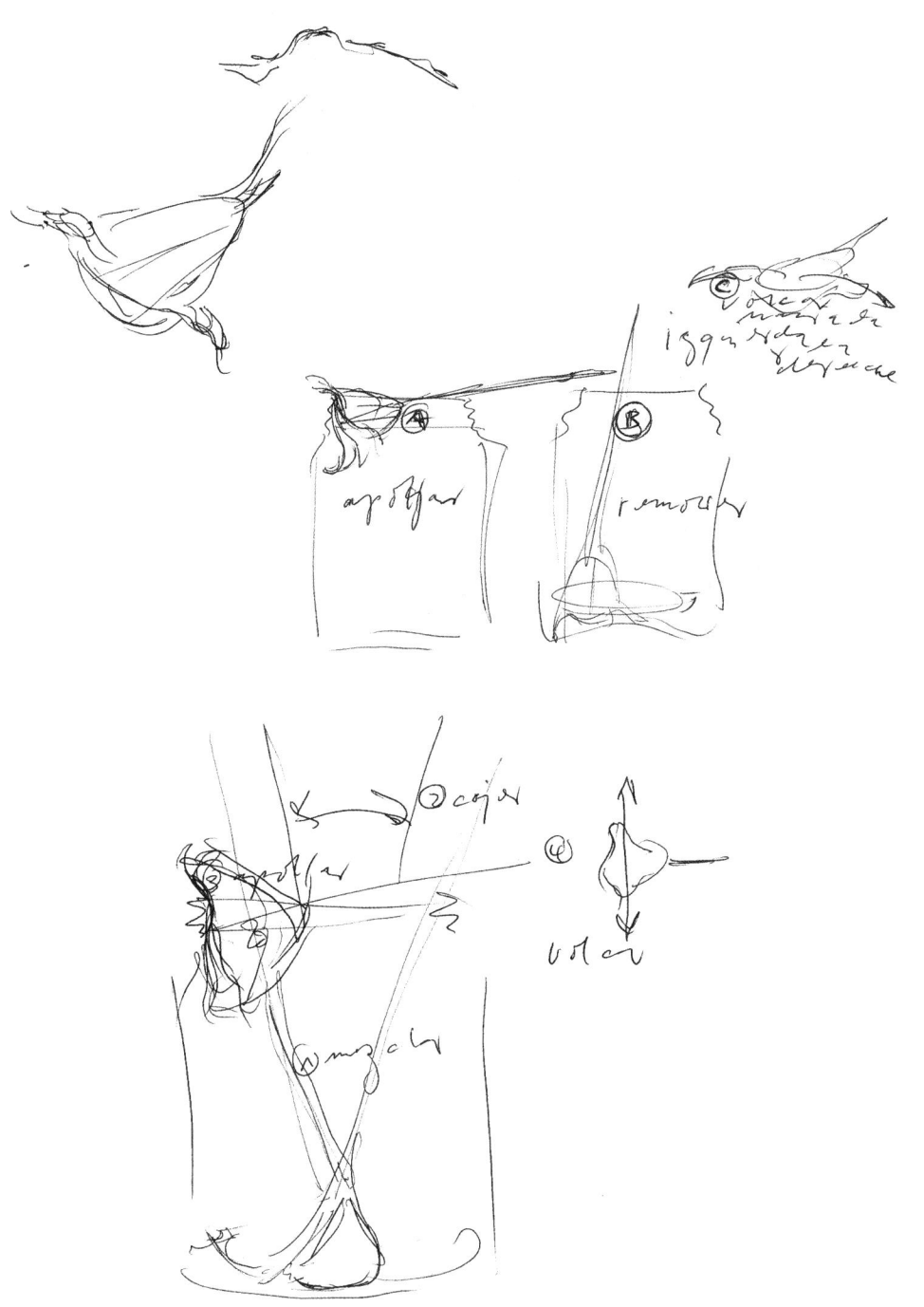

Et cetera

1   Candyfloss burnt with a crème brûlée iron

2   Double sphere imitating a peanut

3   Veal nitro-noodle

4   Martini glass-shaped lollipop

5   Cocktail lollipop

6   Soft caramel tattoo

7   Jelly filling for spring onion

8   elBulliceps mushroom stamp

9   Capsule menu

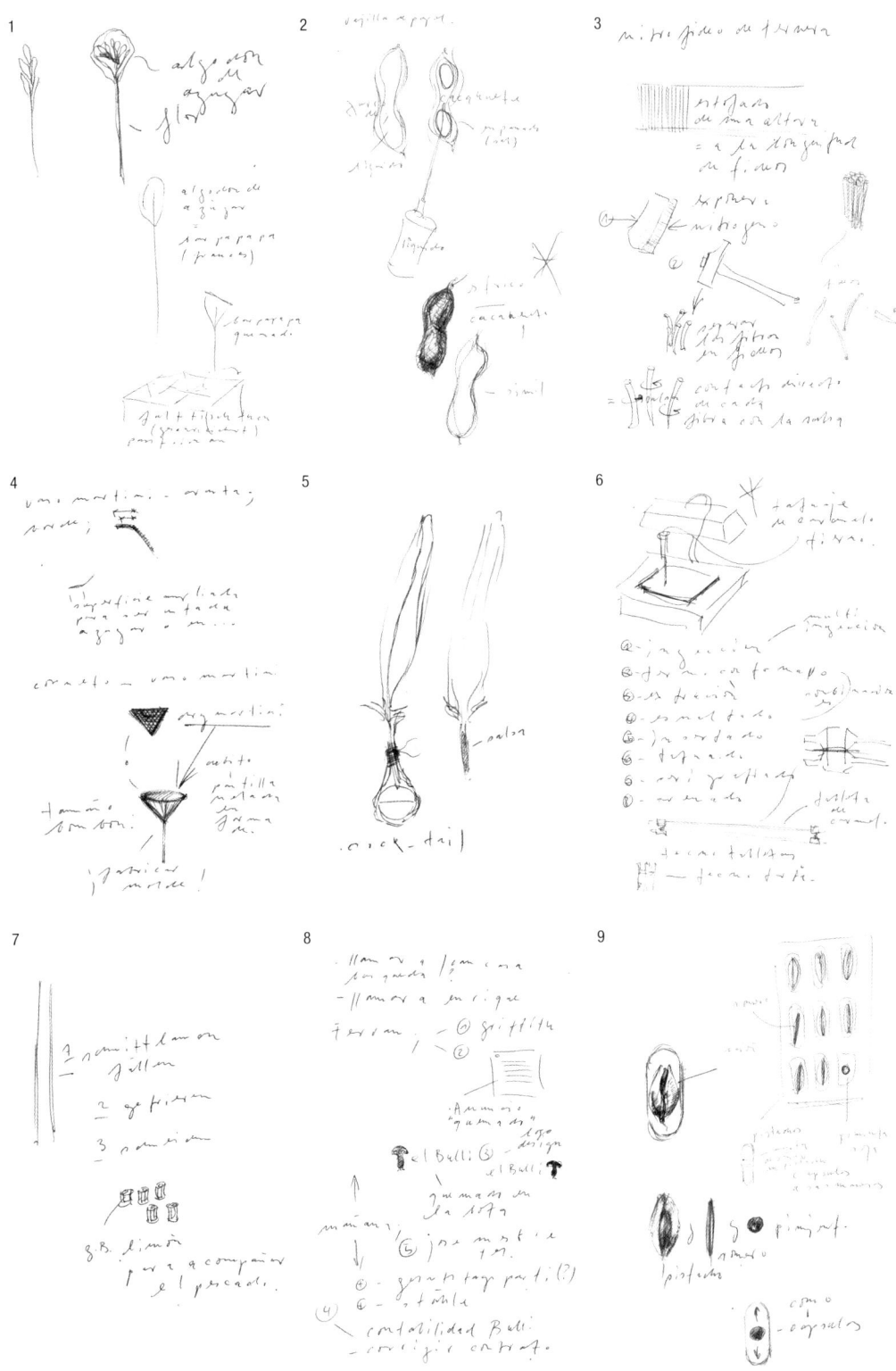

Sketch vinaigrette spoon for Borges

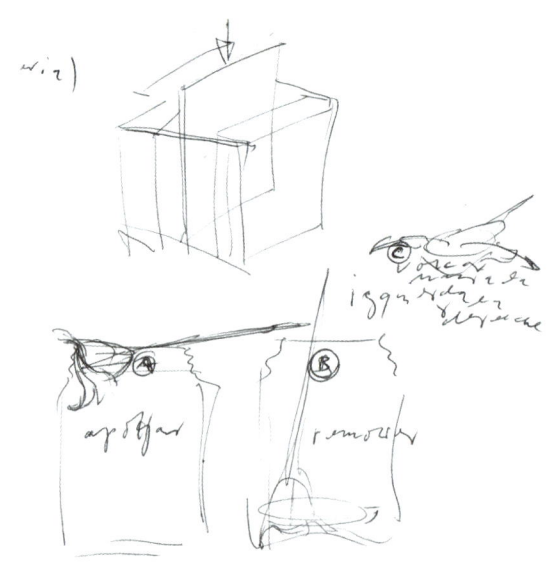

Commercial *spaghetto* kit

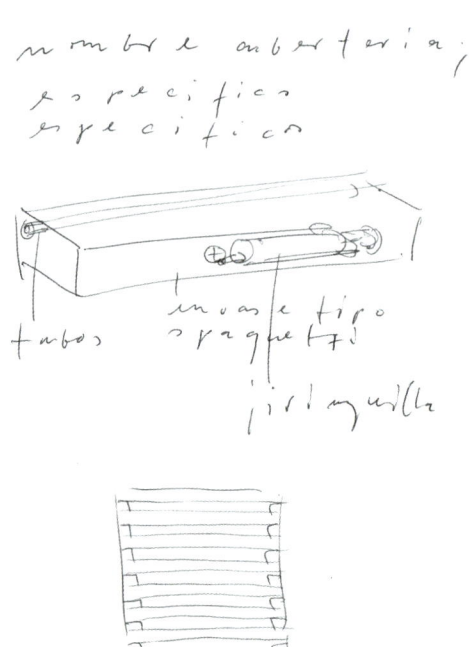

Sea foam nasal spray

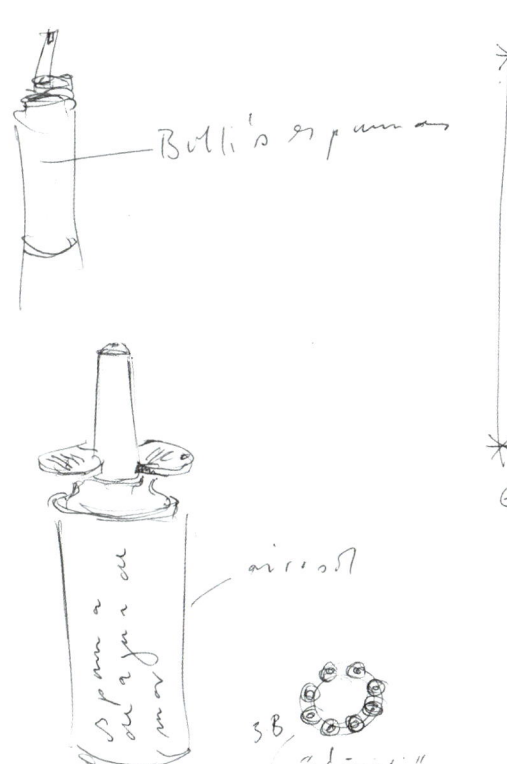

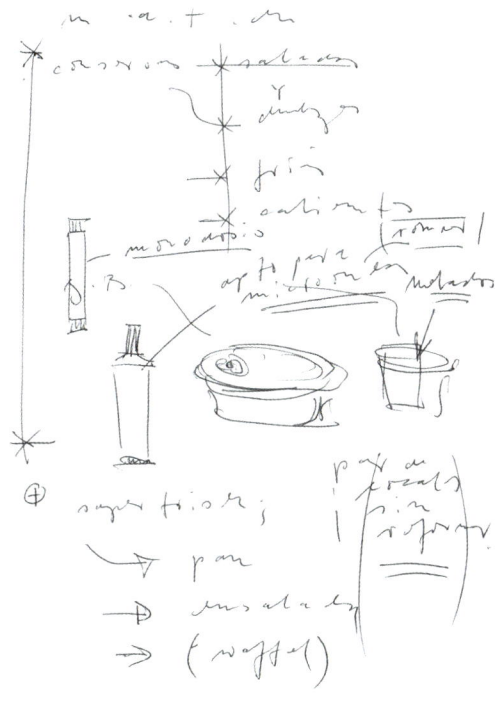

Sketches for *D-Day* exhibition at the Centre Georges-Pompidou

We were invited in 2005 to take part in an exhibition named 'D-Day, le design aujourd'hui', held at the Centre Georges-Pompidou in Paris, to explain the collaboration between design and haute cuisine.

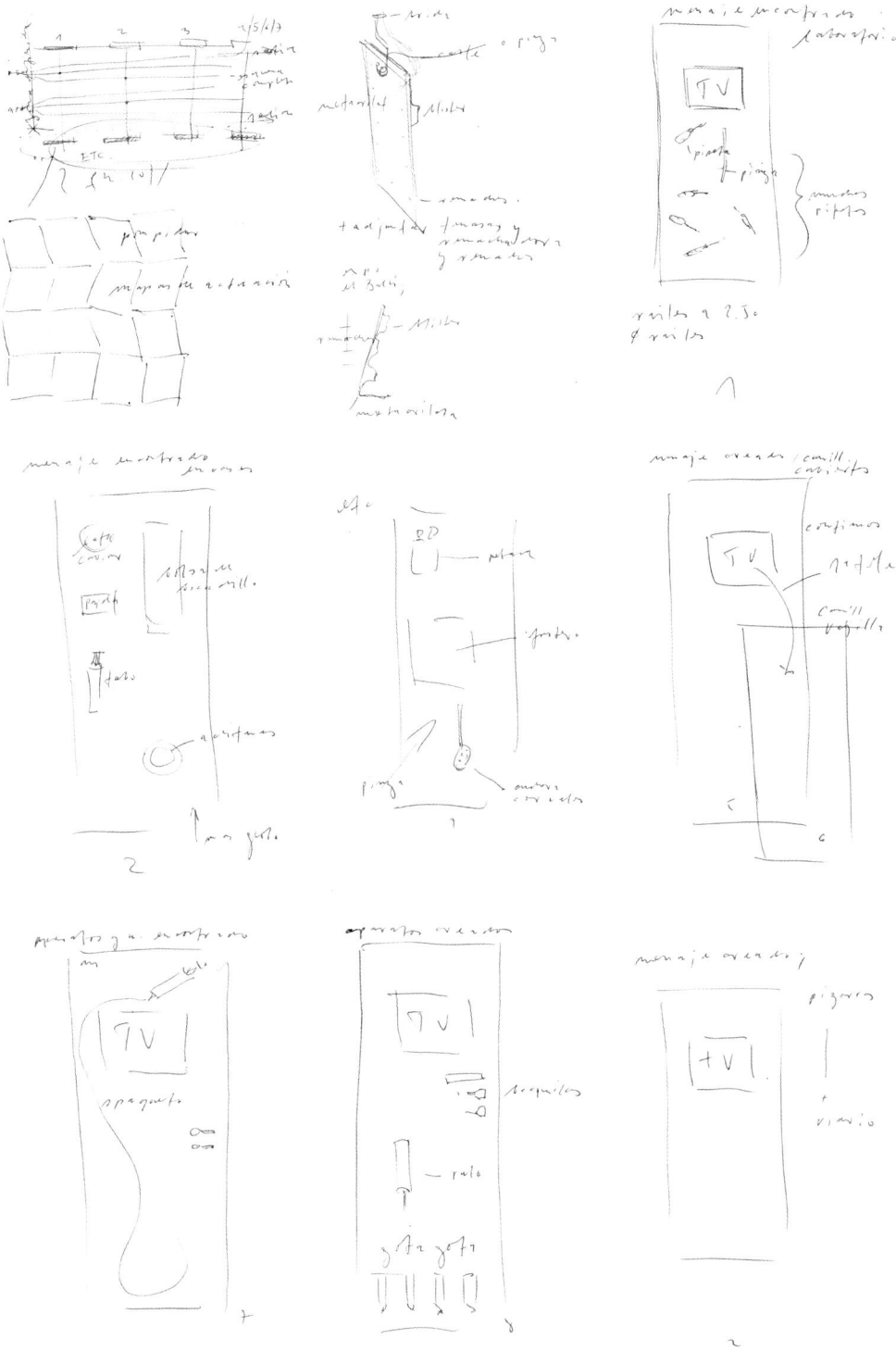

D-Day exhibition at the Centre Georges-Pompidou

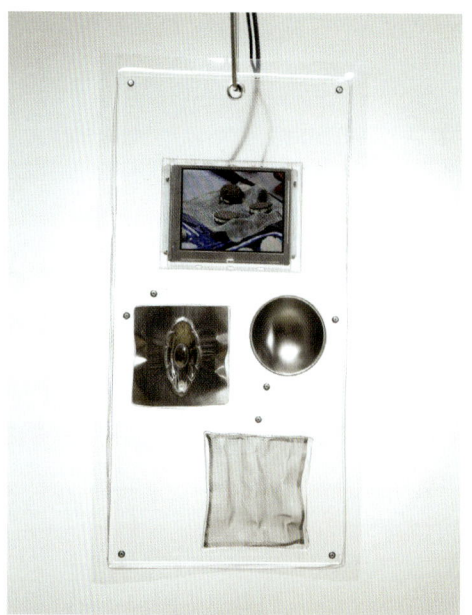
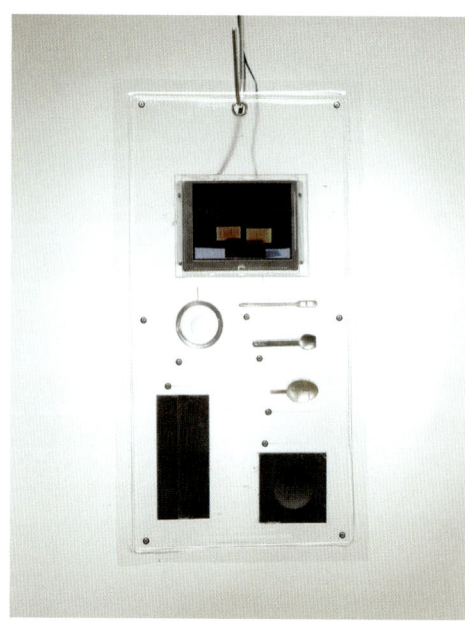

Alicia Foundation

I accompanied Ferran and Albert on their first visits to Món Sant Benet, which would later become the headquarters of the Alicia Foundation. These sketches correspond to the initial stage, and were the result of imagining the form and operation of the foundation.

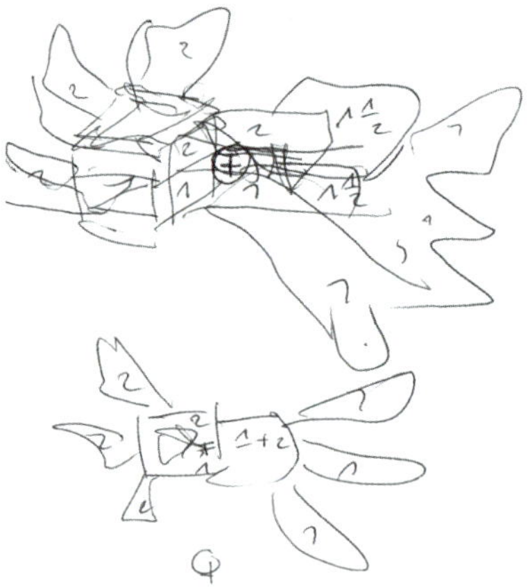

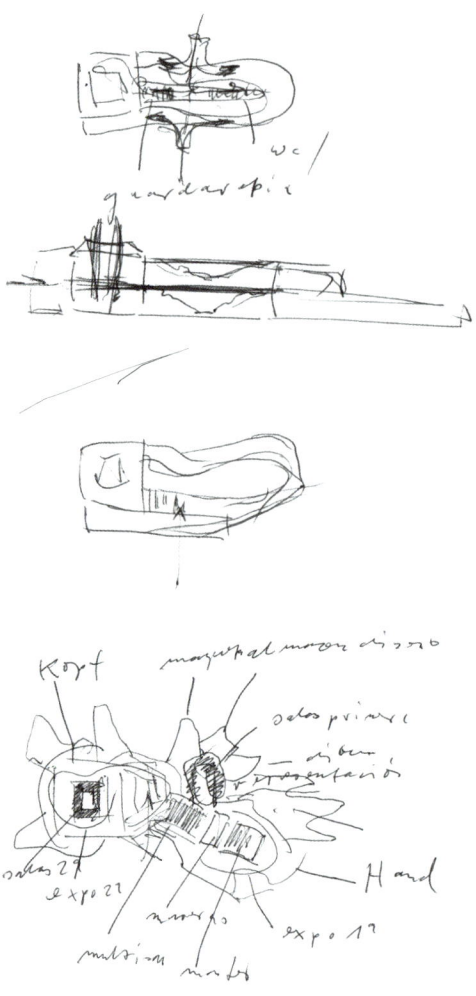

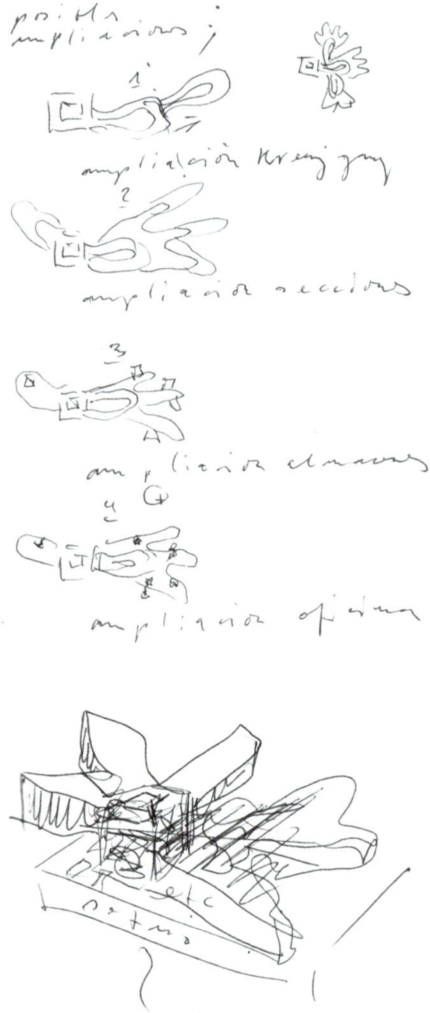

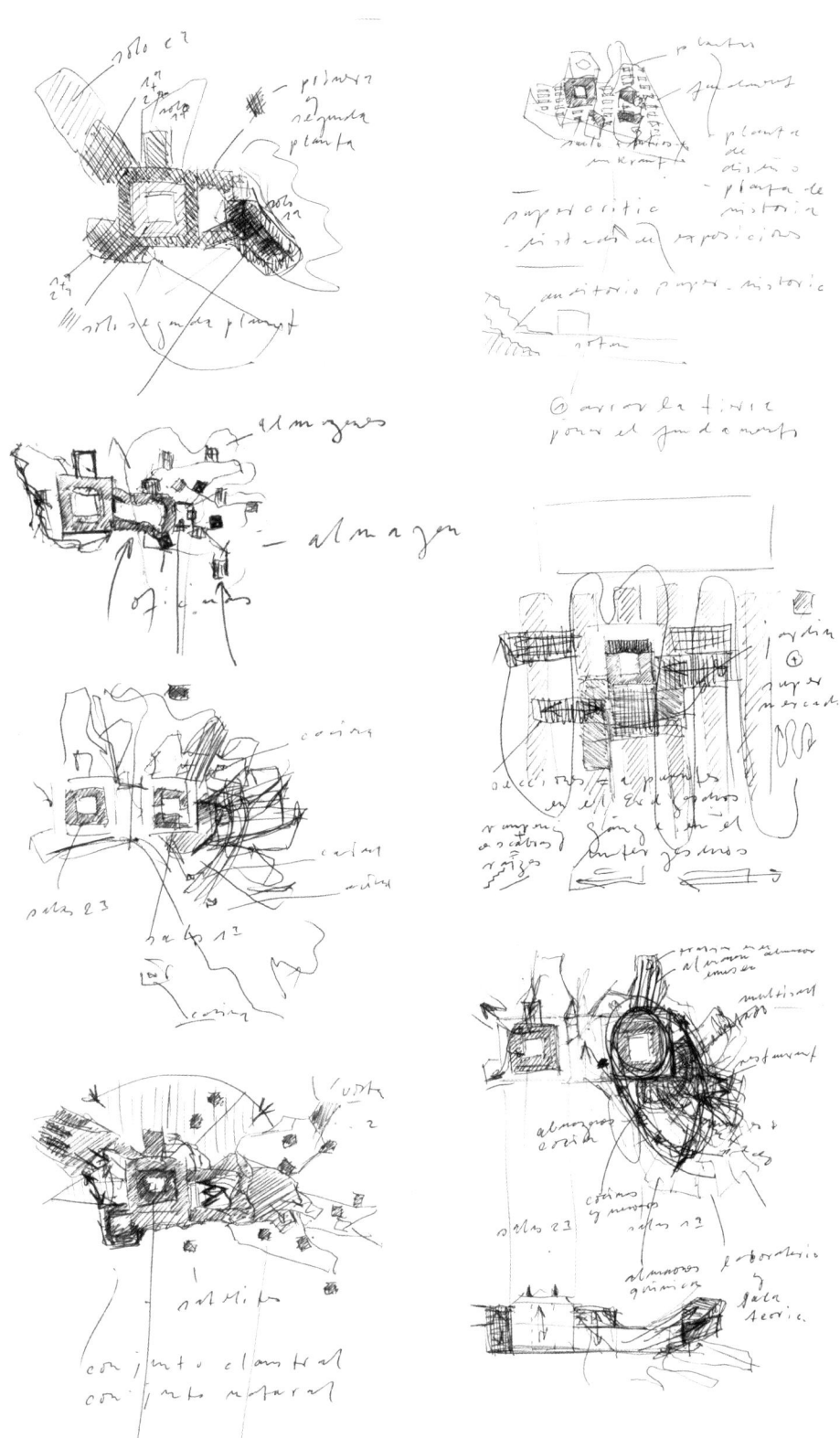

Faces

A sketchbook whose pages reflect what went on during the day, in which a sketch associated with a professional activity might immediately precede a personal drawing. I have the custom of finishing the day by drawing an invented face, which doesn't belong to anybody in particular. Throughout my time at elBulli, I went through sixty sketchbooks in which I found a large number of these drawn faces.

Epilogue

Luki Huber

Twelve years after I stopped working with Ferran Adrià (at least as a full-time job, seeing as we've collaborated on certain occasions since then), some reflections come to mind, together with a couple of questions.

The first of these is: what did I imagine my future as an industrial designer would be like once I'd left Cala Montjoi? In fact, during the entire collaboration with Ferran, I dreamt that at some point the stars would align and I could have something mass produced. Why?

I'd like to explain something about my time before elBulli. The first design I made with my wife, Marta Méndez Blaya, was for candles in the form of origami boats. As soon as we'd finished designing them, we recalled an oath we had both taken: as soon as we had our first solid idea, we were going to show it to a manufacturer. As this idea corresponded to the candles, we visited a manufacturer, who loved the project and offered us three solutions. The first was to buy the idea from us for a lump sum. The second was to pay us royalties on the candles that were produced. The third was that he would manufacture the candles for us, and we would buy them and distribute them ourselves.

The third option was very difficult to pull off, seeing as we lacked the means and infrastructure to distribute the product adequately. We decided on the royalties option, because if the project got off the ground, we'd all benefit. This had a great impact on me, because I saw royalties as the mark of a designer's financial success. This is actually common practice in the world of design. The work involved in design costs the same, whether you sell a lot or a little; which is why I wanted to work with royalties.

As a result, during the part of my career spent with Ferran, I'd always thought that we might be able to mass produce something. But it wasn't to be. The closest we came to this ideal was the Faces series. We could also have achieved it through the triangle of Luesma Vega, Ferran and myself. At that time, we could have said to ourselves: this works at elBulli; let's produce stuff for others, too.

But this didn't happen, and this is where my second question comes in: where did it take me as a professional being part of the staff of a restaurant such as elBulli for so long? As it was, the immediate dream I had of a product that would start to earn royalties never happened, but there's no doubt that my time with Ferran influenced my career as a designer and brought me very significant results. The fact of having worked at elBulli meant that, suddenly, I had credibility in the world that revolved around gastronomy. And on my part, I could be confident of my experience and knowledge.

Because if you spend five years in a kitchen and suddenly have to design pots and pans for a kitchen, you immediately know what makes sense and what doesn't. And this was highly beneficial for me in my work with Lékué, which began in 2005. When they offered me this project, I had a clear idea that I was going to design innovative and functional products. For an object designed for a kitchen to be functional, I insist, it has to make sense in a kitchen, coincide with a real need. Then it occurred to me to ask Ferran if he could provide me with a list of the techniques applied to food that I'd seen at elBulli.

For me, the starting point for designing was very simple: on the one hand, I had to study the list; and on the other, I had to take into consideration the qualities of silicone, which was the basic material with which Lékué worked. These qualities (hygiene, heat resistance, playful/aesthetic value, flexibility, air/water-tightness, lightness, safety, etc.) were perfectly suited to a large number of the techniques that appeared on the list. I read, for instance, cooking en papillote. It made sense, and that's how the Lékué steam case came about. Another example was squeezing, and from this technique came the lemon press, which was based on the flexibility of silicone.

Moreover, while at elBulli, not only did I have the opportunity to come into contact with a world that was totally new to me – haute cuisine – but I was able to discover a way of working that was highly organised and methodical, a quality that is of huge interest to an industrial designer. I believe that in my nature is the quest for rationalisation of work, of meticulousness, but Ferran taught me to ask myself whether it's still possible to improve the method of work.

When I left elBulli, I set up a system of wires in my first studio from which all of the projects that were under way would be hung on sheets of DIN A4 paper. It was a way of always keeping track of what we were doing, so that nothing would be mislaid. And yet... Nonetheless, when I would arrive at the studio on Monday, I would find it tiring to have everything out in the open. It was like being hit by a hammer.

It made sense at elBulli to have every idea out in plain sight, on their typical polystyrene panels, but in my world, because I had to juggle different projects, it was very stressful to have it all in front of you at all times. Hence the need for a selective viewing process, which is perhaps the germ behind the Manual Thinking map. Because I can fold a map or I can leave it attached to one of the panels, which I can later file away in panel storage cabinets, allowing me to only take out what interests me.

However, Manual Thinking isn't only about maps and labels, but also workshops and spaces. The latter concept is derived from the methodical work we've always intended to implement. Our current obsession is not only to help people with the Manual Thinking tool, but to design spaces for creative teamwork, a fact that developed out of my work at elBulli. As I've said on other occasions, a restaurant is an excellent place for creative work. Because creativity with food has to be systematic if it is going to be worthwhile and lasting; because it is necessary to be very effective; because in a restaurant, there is very little time between when an idea is born and its experimental stage; because you work on your feet, without a designated space in which to sit. All of this is conducive to great

flexibility and mental agility, facilitating all the possibilities for association between the participants, and all interactions and synergies. And this spirit is what we intend to apply to Manual Thinking spaces.

The fact of the matter is that among the many objects I designed during my time at elBulli, none of them made the move to industrial production nor earned me any royalties. But the experience I took with me from Cala Montjoi seems to me today to be much greater, and it has left an important mark on me and my career. And this leads me to think of something else, an important factor: the fact of having been through such an atypical collaboration as that which I experienced during those five years ended up giving me total freedom to approach my work as a designer. Plainly speaking, penetrating into a world so decidedly different from the work of an industrial designer taught me that I can do whatever I please. And naturally, this is something I recommend to any professional who works in a creative field.

Published in 2019 by
Grub Street
4 Rainham Close
London
SW11 6SS

Email: food@grubstreet.co.uk
Web: www.grubstreet.co.uk
Twitter: @grub_street
Facebook: Grub Street Publishing

Published originally in Spanish as
Diseños y esbozos para elBulli

A CIP catalogue record for this book is available
from the British Library.

ISBN 978-1-11621-36-2

The moral right of the author has been asserted.

Printed and bound in Slovenia

Project editor:
Mireia Trius / Zahorí de Ideas
www.zahorideideas.com

Text:
**Luki Huber, Josep Maria Pinto,
Trinitat Gilbert**

Design and layout:
Tomoko Sakamoto

Cover design:
Jorge Sagradas

List of photographs:
Francesc Guillamet / elBulliarxiu
Cover, p. 5, 7-8, 11, 12-14, 19, 27-29, 33,
35, 43-44, 45 (↑), 46, 49-51, 55-59, 63-69,
72-73, 79, 81, 103, 109-111, 119, 127,
130-131, 132(←↓), 133(←), 151, 157, 167,
169, 173, 175, 179, 183, 191, 199, 213, 215,
219, 223-227, 239, 240, 245, 249, 251, 257,
262-263, 266, 270, 304, 310-311

Pepo Segura / elBulliarxiu
p. 15

Guillem Trius
p. 10, 16(↘), 17, 29(✓), 36, 45(↓), 47, 80,
83-89, 94-99, 104-107, 112-114, 122,
124-125, 135, 138, 141, 166, 178, 182, 188,
192-193, 197, 214, 218, 238, 241, 250, 253,
267, 271, 276(←), 277, 300
Manual Thinking
p. 6, 9, 16(↑←), 71, 91-93, 123, 129, 132(→),
133(→), 162, 187, 276(↑)

Sketches:
Luki Huber
and **Marta Méndez Blaya** p. 65